ONE BIG PARTY

TO KEEP CANADA INDEPENDENT

Other Books by the Same Author

Agenda: A Plan for Action (1971)

Exit Inflation (1981)

Jobs For All: Capitalism on Trial (1984)

Canada at the Crossroads (1990)

Damn the Torpedoes (1990)

Funny Money:
A Common Sense Alternative to Mainline Economics (1994)

Surviving the Global Financial Crisis:
The Economics of Hope for Generation X (1996)

Arundel Lodge: A Little Bit of Old Muskoka (1996)

The Evil Empire: Globalization's Darker Side (1997)

Stop: Think (1999)

Goodbye Canada (2001) / Adieu Canada (2002)

ONE BIG PARTY

TO KEEP CANADA INDEPENDENT

PAUL T. HELLYER

Chimo Media

National Library of Canada Cataloguing in Publication

Hellyer, Paul, 1923-
  One Big Party: To Keep Canada Independent / Paul Hellyer

Includes bibliographical references and index.
ISBN 0-9733116-0-6

1. Canada – Politics and Government – 1993. 2. Canada – Economic Conditions. 3. Canada – Social Conditions – 1991. I. Title.

FC635.H46 2003   971.064'8   C2003-904680-X

Printed and bound in Canada. The paper used in this book is acid free.

Chimo Media Inc.
99 Atlantic Ave., Suite 302
Toronto, ON M6K 3J8
Tel: (416) 535-0514
Fax: (416) 535-6325

CONTENTS

Acknowledgements   vii

Introduction   viii

1.   From One Evil Empire To Another   1

2.   The War on Iraq   11

3.   American Values and Interests   24

4.   A Compass in Need of Repair   34

5.   Leadership Lost   48

6.   Wall Street and the Axis of Evil   61

7.   Where Does Money Come From?   75

8.   The Banks Play Monopoly   87

9.   Mulroney's Sizzle is a Fizzle   102

10.   Defence and Foreign Policy   124

11.   A World of Hope   142

12.   Why Paul Martin Won't Do   157

13.   A Real Northern Tiger   169

14.   One Big Party   179

Notes   185

Appendix A   193

Bibliography   198

Index   199

For

All Canadian children and grandchildren
who deserve to have the choice
of growing up and living
in
an independent country called Canada.

ACKNOWLEDGEMENTS

A number of individuals have assisted in the preparation of this book.

I am indebted to Catherine Hellyer, Peter Hellyer, and all four members of my staff for reading the draft manuscript. Their comments and suggestions were of great value. They also noted a number of errors and omissions. Responsibility for those that slipped through the net, and for the views expressed in the book, are mine alone.

My thanks to Brian Bacon for providing important material at precisely the right moment; also to Tim Schobert of the Library of Parliament and Charles Rhéame of the Department of National Defence, Directorate of History and Heritage, for their courtesy and cooperation.

Pierre Shapiro gets credit for the cover concept and Lynda Powell for converting the idea into an image of hope for Canada.

Once again I am indebted to Christopher Blackburn for preparing the index in such a professional manner; also for noting a number of errors in need of correction.

As always, my executive assistant, Nina Moskaliuk, deserves special mention for preparing and revising the text, as well as checking the innumerable references.

John Lambersky deserves a citation for his genius in digging out facts and figures from the internet and other sources virtually on demand. Without him the book would have taken twice as long to complete. His gentle but careful editing is also much appreciated.

I am also deeply grateful to Kevin Peck for the workmanlike manner in which he prepared the pages for printing.

Finally, my profound thanks to my wife, Ellen. Nothing I can say would compensate her for the sacrifice she was asked to make.

INTRODUCTION

I like Americans – at least most of them. They are warm, hospitable, industrious, and ingenious people who have pushed the frontiers of industry and commerce to new limits. They have also extended the boundaries of scientific discovery in many areas of great potential benefit to mankind.

A nation comprised of people from many races and religions, Americans have been richly blessed. They occupy one of the most beautiful and productive pieces of real estate on earth. They have become immensely wealthy to an extent far beyond their real needs, though the distribution of that wealth leaves much to be desired.

They are, at the same time, a naïve people, something like us Canadians, and easily convinced by the latest "spin" their government aims in their direction through the mass media. I call the media the weapons of mass intellectual destruction. Their power is sufficient to prove that black is white and that evil is good.

Despite their naivety, my problem is not with the American people; it is with the governments they elect. The U.S. democratic process has been hijacked by an elite group whose policies and plans are unrepresentative of the U.S. population, and inevitably antithetical to long-term American interests. President Eisenhower described them as the industrial-military complex. Increasingly this group of high rollers has been pushing poor countries and poor people around to satisfy their lust for greater power and wealth. This has become an integral aspect of U.S. foreign policy.

With the election of the G.W. Bush administration, however, the trait has escalated to a new order of magnitude. The details were developed in the Project for the New American Century (PNAC). In essence it is the establishment of an American empire by military means. Iraq was just the trial run against a weak and demoralized regime which posed absolutely no immediate threat to the United States. The alleged existence of weapons of mass destruction was just the excuse required to provide justification for the attack under international law.

The small Pentagon clique, who are now running the United States, didn't care about international law. They wanted to establish a new benchmark, namely, an open season on any country that isn't run to the satisfaction of the Pentagon planners and which lacks significant deterrent capability to fight back.

United States foreign policy is now determined by the Pentagon instead of the State Department. It is a classic case of the military tail wagging the foreign policy dog. Nor is there any relief in sight. At the same time that the potential to produce weapons of mass destruction is being portrayed as legitimate license to attack any country, the U.S. Defense Department is developing weapons too evil for description.

The National Missile Defense program is being sold as a protection against missiles launched by rogue states. It is in fact a step in the direction of the installation of U.S. based weapons of mass destruction in space, with a potential ranging from zapping a single individual human person, to wiping out a whole nation.

At a press conference when announcing U.S. rejection of the Kyoto Accord, President George W. Bush said, "A friend is someone who tells you the truth." The truth is that the American foreign and defense policy put into place by his administration is intrinsically evil. And no real friend, as opposed to wimps wallowing in fear, would have anything good to say about it.

Certainly no country that was a real friend would either endorse it or be part of it. They would speak the truth and pray for the day when there is a regime change in the U.S.

That is the reason for this book. Canada is being drawn into the American orbit and we have to make a choice. Unfortunately, with the current political set-up, we will have no choice. There has to be a reshuffling of the political deck – and now, before the 2004 election.

If we don't act, we will become first a U.S. colony and then, later, the 51st state. This is not in our best interests! It is not in the U.S.'s best interests. America needs a friend to tell it the truth. It would be good for the world to know that we care enough about our friends to preserve our independent decision-making capacity.

Not only that, an independent Canada could, if governed properly, become a shining example for the world. In the final chapter of *One Big Party* I set out a plan that might allow us to achieve that goal. It is the only ray of hope on the political horizon.

CHAPTER 1

FROM ONE EVIL EMPIRE TO ANOTHER

"When all government, domestic and foreign, shall be drawn to Washington as the centre of all power, it will render powerless the checks provided of one government on another, and will become as venal and oppressive as the government from which we separated."

Thomas Jefferson

Although my economic radicalism was the prime motive for entering political life more than half a century ago, fate would determine that my primary effort would be in the field of defence rather than economics. I became deeply involved in the ideology of the Cold War.

From the moment when, as the newly appointed Minister of National Defence, I first visited our troops in Germany in May, 1963, I resolved to increase Canada's small but significant contribution to the North Atlantic Treaty Organization (NATO) forces in Europe. As soon as possible our aging, vulnerable trucks, which had substituted as troop carriers, were replaced by sleek, new M113 armoured personnel carriers. We also purchased mobile Howitzers and other items essential to our assigned tasks.

It was all part of an effort to build up NATO conventional forces strong enough to resist an initial thrust by the Soviet Union – without the necessity of using nuclear weapons with potential consequences too horrendous to imagine. Somehow the spread of communism, with its secret police, denial of civil liberties and inefficient economic system had to be contained.

1

It may have been partly luck that the Soviet Union decided not to test the United States by starting a war that might easily and quickly have presented the option of either losing all Europe to the Soviet system or a nuclear escalation leading to the virtual annihilation of both the U.S. and the U.S.S.R. It was the French fear that given that option the U.S. would chicken out, and sacrifice Europe to save its own skin, that led to the French development of their own independent nuclear capability.

In any event, the deterrent worked and the stalemate continued for decades. In many ways it was good for the world because both communists and capitalists curried the favour of Third World countries and presented their most benign and attractive face.

The standoff did not sit well with the U.S., it seems, because it interfered with grander plans that had to be put on hold. President Ronald Reagan labelled the U.S.S.R. as "The Evil Empire" to stake for his country the high ground of moral superiority. It was a presumption that most of us on this side of the "Iron Curtain" were quite happy to accept. At the time there was no hint that the Soviet Union would soon self-destruct and that our hypothesis would be put to the test.

No one could have been happier than I when the Berlin wall came down. I was one of the few who had crossed it, albeit reluctantly, to escort a Liberal colleague, the late Judy LaMarsh, who was determined to cross at Checkpoint Charlie and who couldn't find anyone else brave enough – or perhaps stupid enough – to risk the wrath of the Canadian government which had expressly forbidden the escapade.

We both survived, despite a few anxious hours when the East Germans had possession of our passports, and went on to become cabinet ministers in the Liberal government of Lester B. Pearson when it was formed in April, 1963. The incident did contribute to a little special poignancy, however, when the wall fell and one section after another of the Iron Curtain came tumbling down.

The elation on our side of the curtain was near universal and quite significant on the other side as one country after another regained its freedom. Nearly everyone believed that it was the dawn of a new era of peace and prosperity for people everywhere.

There was much talk of a peace dividend. Without any enemies of military significance, the Western countries, and the U.S. in particular, could reduce expenditures for armaments and divert the savings to myriad essential priorities including health care, education, environmental protection, including sustainable growth, and the development of new sources of energy to replace fossil fuels. There would also be more money for the arts and the alleviation of poverty and illiteracy on a global basis. The prospects were dazzling in their scope and diversity.

Little did we dream that a small group of U.S. "neo-conservative" ideologues had a vastly different "vision" of the New World Order. The group, which includes U.S. Vice-President Dick Cheney; Defense Secretary Donald Rumsfeld; Paul Wolfowitz, Deputy Secretary of Defense; Douglas Feith, the number three man at the Pentagon; Lewis "Scooter" Libby, a Wolfowitz protégé who is Cheney's Chief of Staff, John R. Bolton, a right-winger assigned to the State Department to keep Secretary of State Colin Powell in check; and Elliott Abrams, recently appointed to head Middle East policy at the National Security Council; envision a world dominated by the U.S. both economically and militarily.[1]

Their plan, now commonly known as the Project for a New American Century, includes preventive wars, in clear violation of international law, regime change wherever and whenever the U.S. desires, and if they can get away with it without excessive casualties, and the establishment of a kind of economic and cultural hegemony with America acting as "constabulary" – their word – globally.

This will be accomplished without authority of the United Nations and without the restraint of existing international treaties. It will involve a military buildup unprecedented in "peacetime" history and could trigger an arms race which is precisely the opposite to the peace dividend that the world had rightly looked forward to.

The Machiavellian scheme involves secret police, the curtailment of civil liberties in defiance of the U.S. constitution, and a moribund economy, operating way below its potential – exactly those features for which the Soviet Union was held in contempt.

One distinction may be that the "vision" is "on the record." Not since *Mein Kampf* in the 1930s has anyone been so open about their intentions. The problem, now, as then, is that decent people refuse to believe that such far-fetched belligerence is planned even when they see it in cold print.

To those of us who have been around long enough to put things in historical context there is no disguising the nature of the beast. The Project for a New American Century is a plan to establish an American Empire unprecedented since the fall of the Roman Empire and with consequences more devastating and demoralizing for more people than the Evil Empire from which we thought we had been liberated.

PROJECT FOR A NEW AMERICAN CENTURY

The initial draft of the Pentagon Document "Defense Planning Guidance" on Post-Cold-War Strategy was dated February 18, 1992. Some of the key sections are as follows.

1. Our first objective is to prevent the re-emergence of a new rival, either on the territory of the former Soviet Union or elsewhere, that poses a threat on the order of that posed formerly by the Soviet Union. This is a dominant consideration underlying the new regional defense strategy and requires that we endeavor to prevent any hostile power from dominating a region whose resources would, under consolidated control, be sufficient to general global power.

2. The U.S. must show the leadership necessary to establish and protect a new order that holds the promise of convincing potential competitors that they need not aspire to a greater role or pursue a more aggressive posture to protect their legitimate interests. In non-defense areas, we must account sufficiently for the interests of the

advanced industrial nations to discourage them from challenging our leadership or seeking to overturn the established political and economic order. We must maintain the mechanisms for deterring competitors from even aspiring to a larger regional or global role.

3. Like the coalition that opposed Iraqi aggression, we should expect future coalitions to be ad hoc assemblies, often not lasting beyond the crisis being confronted, and in many cases carrying only general agreement over the objectives to be accomplished. Nevertheless, the sense that the world order is ultimately backed by the U.S. will be an important stabilizing factor.

4. While the U.S. cannot become the world's policeman, by assuming responsibility for righting every wrong, we will retain the preeminent responsibility for addressing selectively those wrongs which threaten not only our interests, but those of our allies or friends, or which could seriously unsettle international relations.

5. We continue to recognize that collectively the conventional forces of the states formerly comprising the Soviet Union retain the most military potential in all of Eurasia; and we do not dismiss the risks to stability in Europe from a nationalist backlash in Russia or efforts to reincorporate into Russia the newly independent republics of Ukraine, Belarus, and possibly others. ... We must, however, be mindful that democratic change in Russia is now irreversible, and that despite its current travails, Russia will remain the strongest military power in Eurasia and the only power in the world with the capacity of destroying the United States.

6. In the Middle East and Southwest Asia, our overall objective is to remain the predominant outside power in the region and preserve U.S. and Western access to the region's oil.[2]

When a leaked copy of the document prepared under the supervision of Paul Wolfowitz, the Pentagon's Under-Secretary for Policy, was disclosed by the *New York Times* in

March 1992 the negative reaction from both the White House and foreign capitals was so strong that it had to be redrafted.

The new sanitized version adopted a much more conciliatory tone. It stated: "One of the primary tasks we face today in shaping the future is carrying longstanding alliances into the new era, and turning old enmities into new cooperative relationships."[3]

The document made a small bow in the direction of a levelling of military investments coupled with greater economic and security cooperation. The bottom line remained unchanged, however. "It is not in our interest or those of the other democracies to return to earlier periods in which multiple military powers balanced one another off in what passed for security structures, while regional, or even global peace hung in the balance."[4]

As someone who has long observed the techniques of creating politically acceptable language, and a sometimes practitioner of that craft, I would say that the principal difference between the first and revised drafts is in the weasel words. The men responsible and their ideas have changed little if at all.

That conclusion can be substantiated by their actions in office. The abrogation of the anti-ballistic missile treaty, the vast buildup in military expenditures and their plans to put weapons of mass destruction in space.

It all adds up to an irrevocable resolve to maintain the U.S. status as the world's only super-power and to take whatever steps are necessary, including those that may not be necessary but which can be made to appear to be necessary, to that end.

One has to ask how such a small group of neo-conservative ideologues could take over the U.S. Administration as a first step in taking over the world. In a stroke of good luck for them, and bad luck for nearly everyone else including the vast majority of the American people, George W. Bush chose Dick Cheney as his vice-presidential running mate. The die was cast.

Once the Supreme Court decided that George W. Bush would succeed Bill Clinton as the 43rd President of the United

States, the President-elect put the former Defense Secretary in charge of his transition team. So Cheney slotted one after another of his Pentagon team for the New American Century into key posts to the point where they held the balance of power in the incoming administration. Overnight the long-held tenet of defence being an extension of foreign policy was reversed. Henceforth the Defense Department tail would swing the State Department dog.

It may have been relatively easy to persuade President George W. Bush to abandon his stated policy of not getting America more deeply involved in international affairs but persuading the American people would be more difficult. Sophisticated Americans would question such a giant sea change in policy.

The authors of "Rebuilding America's Defenses, Strategy, Forces and Resources for a New Century" recognized this difficulty from the outset. "Further, the process of transformation, even if it brings revolutionary changes, is likely to be a long one, absent some catastrophic and catalyzing event – like a new Pearl Harbor."[5]

Well, it wasn't long before they got their catastrophic and catalyzing event. Terrorists struck the World Trade Center in New York and the Pentagon in Washington.

SEPTEMBER 11, 2001

I wept internally when the full impact of what was happening finally penetrated my consciousness. I was at the office when one of the staff said they had just heard on the radio that the World Trade Center in New York had been attacked. We turned on the TV and there it was – a spiral of flame and smoke escaping from the side of one of the towers.

We have become so familiar with "reality" television in recent years it took a few seconds to absorb the fact that what we were watching was genuine and not some Orwellian computer creation. As we watched in silent horror we could only imagine how awful the reality was.

It was a long day and night which no witness could ever forget. The reports of casualties – the dead and the dying. The firemen trapped inside in the course of duty. The occasional good luck story of someone who had escaped or missed their train to be blessed by fortune.

Almost the whole world mourned.   Canada mourned. The overwhelming majority of Muslims condemned the treacherous attacks. A vast crowd of 80,000 assembled on Parliament Hill in Ottawa in an outpouring of love and affection for our American friends and neighbours. Many of us attended special remembrance services in our respective churches as an expression of deepest concern and sympathy. A group of people from Toronto organized a weekend pilgrimage to New York to demonstrate their support and empathy.

My concern for the friends and families of the injured and dead was genuine and unwavering. My sympathy for the U.S. government began to grow a bit thin, however, when I heard President Bush cite the reasons for the attack. "Why do they hate us,?" he asked rhetorically in an address to the Congress.   "They hate what they see right here in this chamber: a democratically elected government. Their leaders are self-appointed. They hate our freedoms: our freedom of religion, our freedom of speech, our freedom to vote and assemble and disagree with each other."[6]

Contrast that with Osama bin Laden's version.   "Every Muslim must rise to defend his religion. The wind of faith is blowing and the wind of change is blowing to remove evil from the Peninsula of Muhammad, peace be upon him.

"As to America, I say to it and its people a few words: I swear to God that America will not live in peace before peace reigns in Palestine, and before all the army of infidels depart the land of Muhammad, peace be upon him."[7]

In essence he relates the hatred toward America to the presence of U.S. troops near the holy Muslim sites in Saudi Arabia (recently largely withdrawn) and the less than even-handed approach to the Israeli-Palestinian conflict.

Of the two, bin Laden spoke the truth. After all, he was the leader of al-Qaeda and whether he was the principal planner of the 9/11 attack or not, he was well informed concerning the origins of the kind of fanatical hatred of the U.S. which led to such treachery.

President Bush must have known the real reasons. Someone in the State Department, the CIA or the FBI must have told him. Still he never let the American people in on the secret. To do so would have created too much disillusionment. More important it would have undermined the plans of his advisers to implement the Project for a New American Century.

Months later the President was forced to admit that he had been forewarned of a possible al-Qaeda hijacking plot nearly a month before September 11, 2001. "U.S. National Security Adviser Condoleezza Rice acknowledged that the White House was alerted that 'something was coming' and that Mr. Bush was alerted to the possibility of hijackings in a written 'analytical' briefing delivered to him at his ranch in Crawford, Texas, on August 6."[8] She went on to insist that there was no information about the time, place or method of the attack.

There are doubters who believe that someone in the administration knew more than has been admitted. Michel Chossudovsky, economics professor at the University of Ottawa and author of *War and Globalisation: The Truth Behind September 11*, is one.[9] He suggests that it may not have been mere coincidence that the Pakistani head of Inter-Services Intelligence, Lieutenant-General Mahmood Ahmed, with close ties to both Osama bin Laden and the CIA, visited Washington in September of 2001. Other questions arise such as those raised by *Toronto Star* columnist Michele Landsberg after watching a video entitled "The Great Deception," produced by Barrie Zwicker, a *Globe and Mail* colleague from her youth.

"Why did the two squadrons of fighter jets at Andrews Air Force base, 19 kilometres from Washington, not zoom into action to defend the White House, one of their primary tasks?

"Why did George Bush sit for half an hour in a Florida classroom, listening to a girl talk about her pet goat, after his chief of staff told him about the second plane? For that matter, why did he pretend that he first learned of the attacks in that classroom, when he had actually been briefed as he left his hotel that morning?"[10]

It is doubtful that the truth will ever be known. Scholars and conspiracy theorists are still arguing as to whether or not President Franklin D. Roosevelt had advance notice of the attack on Pearl Harbor in 1941. Certainly it was the key to U.S. engagement in World War II which he had been trying to promote.

The similarity between September 11, 2001 and Pearl Harbor is noteworthy, if inconclusive. It was the key to the "war on terrorism" which is not really a war on terrorism at all. If it were, all that would be necessary is some changes in U.S. foreign policy and more effective intelligence and police operations in cooperation with all countries dedicated to peaceful solutions to problems – which includes the vast majority.

Instead, the "war on terrorism" is a cover for virtually unlimited expansion of American power and influence in accordance with the Project for a New American Century. In bald terms it is a licence for military aggression outside the rules of international law. Already it has permitted the U.S. to attack two countries, Afghanistan and Iraq, which have both been on its "most desired" list of interventions for a long time.

While most friendly observers could understand why a strike on the Taliban might be justified – despite pleas for mercy and reminders that it had been an ally of the U.S. in the Cold War – because it appeared to be essential to get at bin Laden. This despite a Taliban offer to turn bin Laden over if the U.S. could provide evidence of his complicity – an offer that was rejected out of hand.

The war against Iraq, however, is quite different. It was not harbouring al-Qaeda operations and it posed no imminent threat to the United States which is the essential condition for a pre-emptive strike. None of this really mattered. Iraq had been on the Defense Department's hit list for years and the decision to attack was made within weeks of the September 11 tragedy.

CHAPTER 2

THE WAR ON IRAQ

"In the councils of government, we must guard against the acquisition of unwarranted influence, whether sought or unsought, by the military-industrial complex. The potential for the disastrous rise of misplaced power exists and will persist."

Dwight D. Eisenhower

Some months before the beginning of the war on Iraq I just happened to be listening to the radio and heard President George W. Bush use the term "weapons of mass destruction" eight or nine times in the course of three or four minutes.

"Oh, oh," I said to myself, "something's up, that is brainwashing."

It would be impossible to count the number of times that same quote was used by the President and his advisers in the weeks that followed. It didn't take long for everyone to get the point. Saddam Hussein and his Iraqi regime were the possessors of "weapons of mass destruction," and these posed a threat to the United States.

It was only after considerable research that I was able to cut through some of this deliberately created fog and get close to the facts. I found that the decision to invade Iraq must have been taken in the fall of 2001 shortly after the attacks on New York and Washington.

This assertion was voiced by former Israeli Prime Minister Benjamin Netanyahu and published in the *World Tribune* in December, 2001. "They have decided [on Iraq]," Netanyahu told the annual Herzliya Conference on Israeli

11

strategy. "It will not be in the long- term future." He said Bush had decided that Iraq will be the next target in the U.S.-led war on terrorism.[1]

Meanwhile the U.S. armed forces began to gear up for war and the White House and Pentagon spin doctors searched for a plausible excuse. Weapons of mass destruction seemed best to fill that requirement. Ultimately the majority in the U.S. and many others, especially in the English-speaking world, believed them.

Yet the U.S. Administration knew, or should have known, that the Iraqis possessed no nuclear weapons and no capacity to produce them. Furthermore any remnants of chemical or biological capability were of little, if any, consequence long before the war was launched. This represents a profound change in capability compared to that which existed before the Gulf War in 1990. At that time a team of scientists including Imad Khadduri, a former Iraqi nuclear scientist who later emigrated to Canada and now lives north of Toronto, was making good progress toward developing a nuclear capability. Following the Gulf War, however, funding was terminated and the team dispersed.

Prior to the war on Iraq, Khadduri insisted that Iraq had neither the scientific expertise nor the hardware to produce a nuclear bomb. That was in stark contrast to George W. Bush's claim that Iraq represented a credible nuclear threat – a claim Khadduri called "ridiculous."[2]

With respect to chemical and bacteriological weapons the U.S. was on more familiar ground in the knowledge that the Iraqis' capability had its roots in the U.S. A report of the United States Senate Committee on Banking, Housing and Urban Affairs included the following:

"We contacted a principal supplier of these materials to determine what, if any, materials were exported to Iraq which might have contributed to an offensive or defensive biological warfare program. Records available from the supplier for the period from 1985 until the present show that during this time, pathogenic (meaning 'disease producing'), toxigenic (meaning 'poisonous'), and other biological research materials were exported to Iraq pursuant to application and licensing by the

U.S. Department of Commerce. Records prior to 1985 were not available, according to the supplier. These exported biological materials were not attenuated or weakened and were capable of reproduction."[3]

It is clear that the U.S. had been exporting the ingredients for biological warfare to Iraq prior to 1985. The list included:

- **Bacillus anthracis** (anthrax)
- **Clostridium bolulinum**
- **Histoplasma capsulatum** (causes a disease super-ficially resembling tuberculosis)
- **Brucella melitensis** (a bacteria which can cause chronic fatigue, loss of appetite, profuse   sweating when at rest, pain in joint and muscles, insomnia, nausea, and damage to major organs)
- **Clostridium perfringens** (a highly toxic bacteria which causes gas gangrene)
- In addition, several shipments of **Escherichia Coli** (E. Coli) and genetic materials, as well as human and bacterial DNA, were shipped directly to the Iraq Atomic Energy Commission.[4]

Saddam Hussein used chemical weapons against Iran in 1983 and 1984 with the implicit approval of the U.S. An estimated 20,000 Iranians were killed by mustard gas and the nerve agents tabun and sarin. Later, Iraq used chemical weapons in its genocide campaign against the Kurds in September of 1988.[5]

In the fall of 2002 the London *Observer* reflected on the American attitude at the time.

"As Iraq's use of poison gases in war and peace was public knowledge, the question arises: what did the United States Administration do about it then? Absolutely nothing. Indeed, so powerful was the grip of the pro-Baghdad lobby on the Administration of Republican President Ronald Reagan that it got the White House to foil the Senate's attempt to penalise Iraq for its violation of the Geneva Protocol on Chemical Weapons to which it was a signatory. This made Saddam believe that the U.S. was his firm ally – a deduction that paved the way for his brutal invasion and occupation of Kuwait and the 1991 Gulf War."[6]

It was the Gulf War which led, ultimately, to Saddam Hussein's downfall. The U.N. imposed conditions for dismantling Iraq's nuclear, chemical and biological capability, together with constant bombing by British and U.S. air forces, reduced Iraq's once formidable capability to near-total impotence. One has to assume, therefore, that U.K. and U.S. insistence that "weapons of mass destruction" remained a threat was primarily political propaganda without backing by any hard and credible intelligence.

Former U.S. Marine Corps intelligence officer and then U.N. weapons inspector in Iraq, Scott Ritter, appeared to be the most credible witness. A card-carrying Republican, who voted for George W. Bush in 2002, he cannot be accused of political bias.

This is what he told CNN in London, England, in July, 2002.

"Well look: As of December 1998 we had accounted for 90 to 95 percent of Iraq's weapons of mass destruction capability – 'we' being the weapons inspectors.

"We destroyed all the factories, all of the means of production and we couldn't account for some of the weaponry, but chemical weapons have a shelf-life of five years. Biological weapons have a shelf-life of three years. To have weapons today, they would have had to rebuild the factories and start the process of producing these weapons since December 1998."[7]

When asked how we knew that hasn't been happening, Ritter replied:

"We don't, but we cannot go to war on guesswork, hypothesis and speculation. We go to war on hardened fact. So Tony Blair says he has a dossier; present the dossier. George W. Bush and his Administration say they know with certainty; show us how you know."[8]

The essence of Ritter's evidence was confirmed by the United Nations but this had no effect on the people who had already decided to go to war and were only interested in conditioning public opinion to accept their word that there was a valid reason for it.

In fact the whole exercise of trying to get U.N. Security Council backing for the war was nothing but a charade – "process" – as we call it in politics. Tony Blair decided that it would shore up his precarious position in the British Labour Party if the project carried U.N. approval. The reluctant Bush, desperate for support that would lend credibility to his proposed adventure, agreed.

The effort backfired when France, Germany and Russia, three of Europe's significant powers, rebelled. They realized only too well what the U.S. was up to and that the public reasons for the conflict were spurious. They also knew that the U.S. would be the principal beneficiary and that there would be no advantage for them. On the contrary, their relative advantage would be diminished. So, like the U.S., they played power politics.

LESSONS FROM HISTORY

As hope of a U.N. stamp of approval began to fade it was fascinating to watch as new justifications for war were thrown into the public relations brew. Remember the 1930s, we were told, when the old League of Nations sat idly by and watched the German army move first to annex Austria, in March, 1938, and the Sudentenland, the German-inhabited border area of Czechoslovakia, in October.[9] The name of the United Kingdom Prime Minister Neville Chamberlain, and his alleged "peace at any price" policy, was recalled.

I didn't know whether to laugh or cry when many of my friends and acquaintances bought this argument and threw it in my face. If only the allies had acted more quickly, things might have been different. So we should learn from history and stop Saddam Hussein before he overruns one country after another.

Indeed, we should learn from history; but my take on the analogy would be quite different. In the 1930s it was Germany that had the world's most powerful army and air force and the most technologically sophisticated weaponry. What country enjoys comparable military superiority in

2003?   Certainly not Iraq, with its pitifully inadequate weaponry. If one wants to pursue the 1930s analogy, it is not far-fetched to suggest that Afghanistan and Iraq have something in common with Austria and the Sudentenland.

While it is difficult for those of us who have enjoyed a long and friendly relationship with the U.S. to accept the implications of such historical parallels, we would be fools not to look beyond the rhetoric of the moment and remind ourselves of the U.S. ruling clique's published intentions. It is not a happy read.

A supplementary "reason" given for the war on Iraq was to remove a ruthless dictator, guilty of myriad crimes, from power. Okay, so Saddam Hussein is a blackguard. There is no contest here. He has used poison gas on his own people, mutilated or killed thousands of political opponents and ruled through absolute terror.

But he had done all of these horrible things when he was still America's friend and ally against Iran. Yet there were no sanctions then.   And American firms were allowed to supply this despot with the weapons of war including "weapons of mass destruction." So why the belated outrage, and why was Saddam singled out for special attention when there was a whole rogues' gallery of dictators to choose from?

Muammar Gaddafi, of Libya, has sponsored terrorism for decades and was deemed responsible for the Lockerbie tragedy; Alexander Lukashenko, of Belarus, Europe's last dictator, dissolved parliament, uses the KGB to intimidate opponents, and represses free speech and freedom of the press; Robert Mugabe of Zimbabwe, has been accused of corruption, the seizure of white farmers' land; and, of course, North Korea's Kim Jong-il, amongst others.

Of these Kim Jong-il is unique, in the sense that he is the only one who admits that he is developing a nuclear capability.   So if weapons of mass destruction were the distinguishing feature between acceptable dictators and those who were not, Kim Jong-il should have been at the top of the list.   Instead, Bush consistently brushed this threat aside, saying that North Korea was simply "back to the old blackmail game."[10]

The U.S. has a long history of selectively choosing between good and bad dictators. It supported the iron rule of the Shah of Iran prior to his overthrow by the Ayatollah Khomeni. It also preferred the Chilean dictator Augusta Pinochet to the democratically elected government of Salvadore Allende, which CIA agents and their collaborators helped to overthrow. There are many more examples that could be cited but these two are sufficient to justify extreme cynicism in respect of the post-war claims concerning the purpose of the conflict.

Gary Milhollin, Director of the Wisconsin Project on Nuclear Arms Control, and Executive Editor of Iraqwatch.org, was in Iraq looking for signs of the weapons of mass destruction which allegedly posed the clear and imminent threat to the United States, and which had been given as the justification for a preventive strike. He was clearly embarrassed when no evidence came to light. He was contacted by the CBC radio show "As it Happens" on May 12, 2003 to discuss the situation.

When asked how embarrassing the situation is, he replied: "It's very embarrassing internationally. We told the countries that came into the war with us and we told the whole world that we were doing this to prevent the threat of weapons of mass destruction against U.S. citizens and citizens of other countries – and we simply aren't finding any. ... Either we were misled, which I'm beginning to think we were, or this stuff has just evaporated into thin air."[11]

When asked who would mislead the public, he replied: "I think it has to be at the decision-making level of the U.S. government. If our intelligence was solid enough to take us into a war, then it should be solid enough to find the evidence we are looking for. And if we don't find it then I think it's fair to be skeptical about how solid it was in the first place."[12] (This is exactly the position that former U.S. marine officer and U.N. inspector Scott Ritter took before the war began.)

When asked who would be doing the misleading, he replied: "Certainly the Secretary of State, the Secretary of Defense, National Security Advisor ... Cabinet officers would have an obligation, it seems to me, to know whether they have solid information before they go before the world and announce it as a cause of war."[13]

Indeed the Cabinet should have known and senior members probably did know that the truth was insufficient to justify their plans. So they created a "line" designed to do the trick. Not only were the men and women of the U.S. armed forces misled concerning the reasons for the war, so, too, was the American public and others who believed what the White House and the Pentagon were saying. We were collectively brainwashed to believe, as long as that still appeared credible, that the whole war was to protect America and its friends from "weapons of mass destruction." But when that myth was exposed other equally creative reasons were given in order to mask the truth.

The truth is very simple and straightforward. It can be found in the original Defense Planning Guidance on Post-Cold War Strategy of February, 1992, the substance of which was confirmed in later versions of the document. "In the Middle East and Southwest Asia, our overall objective is to remain the predominant outside power in the region and preserve U.S. and Western access to the region's oil."[14]

Nothing could be clearer. It was a war about geopolitics and oil which was what I and others said and wrote from the outset, despite the official camouflage. I wasn't even aware at the time that Defense Secretary Donald Rumsfeld had called for a war on Iraq September 11, 2001, soon after Saudi hijackers attacked the World Trade Center and the Pentagon. This despite the lack of any evidence of a connection between Saddam Hussein's regime and the terrorist attacks. Apparently Rumsfeld could hardly wait to get on with The Project for a New American Century of which he had been an integral part from its inception.[15]

WAR AND PEACE

In the little more than a decade since the Gulf War in 1991 U.S. military technology has improved immeasurably. The use of laser guided bombs linked to satellite communications has tended to limit, though not eliminate, civilian casualties. Sometimes the "smart bombs" miss their targets. And sometimes innocent bystanders are too close to military or strategic targets when the bombs hit.

According to a *Los Angeles Times* survey in the Iraqi capital and its outlying districts, at least 1,700 civilians died and more than 8,000 were injured in the five week period beginning March 20, 2003. In addition, undocumented civilian deaths in Baghdad number at least in the hundreds and could reach 1,000 according to Islamic burial records and humanitarian groups trying to trace those missing in the conflict.[16]

Obviously in a war where one side has such unchallenged air superiority it is relatively easy for ground forces to press forward with minimum resistance. So even without the benefit of a second northern front from Turkey, General Tommy Franks was able to conquer Baghdad in record time. What soon became painfully clear, however, is that despite their unquestioned military skill and superiority the Pentagon planners were woefully unprepared for the challenge of stabilizing the country and maintaining law and order.

Their priorities appeared much too slanted to please many critics. It was duly noted that the oil buildings were carefully protected while hospitals and other buildings essential to the restoration of some kind of normalcy were wide open for looting and destruction.

Then there was worldwide consternation and dismay when U.S. soldiers made no effort to protect the Iraqi National Museum with its priceless treasures dating back to the dawn of civilization. Some artifacts were associated with the era of King Nebuchadnezzar and the Babylonian Empire.

If the military appeared totally unprepared for the post-war requirements, there appeared to be little immediate improvement when the first administrator arrived. The appointment of retired Lt. General Jay Garner may have been another error in judgement. His appointment underlined the ongoing feud between the Pentagon and the State Department. The Pentagon clique were determined to have one of their men in charge.

Mr. Garner did not have the political savvy required for such a delicate post. Reports circulated that he had reappointed senior members of Saddam Hussein's Baathist party as ministers, university administrators and to other high level posts. These appointments undermined the confidence of all of the major Iraqi factions. One could only hope that his successor, L. Paul Bremer III, a career diplomat with close ties to the Pentagon, could do better.

At the time of the transition, after a few weeks of American occupation, the first paragraph of an editorial in the *New York Times* pretty well summed up the situation.

"Lines at the gasoline pumps in Iraq now last up to three days. Electricity, needed for water and refrigeration units, flickers on and off. Uncollected garbage rots in the hot streets. An outbreak of cholera was reported yesterday in Basra. Cases of diarrhea in young children are also increasing. Hospitals looted of drugs and diagnostic equipment limp along. Few Iraqis are feeling nostalgic for the sadistic terror of Saddam Hussein. But in the bad old days, basic services were more dependable."[17]

CHUTZPAH

If the war on Iraq was waged "to remain the predominant outside power in the region" and deny that role to any other foreign power or group of powers, the U.S. displayed unprecedented chutzpah in expecting its friends and allies to help it achieve its goals and pick up part of the tab for the collateral damage resulting from its wars.

Like any flowering Imperial power it has few if any scruples about the methods it employs. Persuasion, bribery, bullying and verbal threats about the possible consequences of non-cooperation comprise a partial inventory of its diplomatic arsenal. The U.S. ambassador to Canada Paul Cellucci's straight-faced sob story that: "We would be there for

Canada, part of our family, and that is why so many in the United States are disappointed and upset that Canada is not fully supporting us now,"[18] took the prize for ingenuity. There is nothing like a good tug at vulnerable heart strings to persuade loyal Canadians to rally to the American cause.

There are many ways the U.S. has been there for Canada. They invaded us in 1776 and again in 1812 and it is good for English-speaking Canadians to be reminded that without the valiant assistance of French-speaking Canadians and the Aboriginals the Americans would not have been repelled and there would be no Canada today.

American Fenians raided Canada in 1866, 1870 and 1871 and there was no effort by the U.S. government to stop their terrorist acts against their northern neighbour. Perhaps the official indifference related to the Alaska boundary dispute which began with the U.S. purchase in 1867. The U.S. refused to accept the boundary stipulated by the treaty in 1825 preferring to rely on Russian maps that showed more land belonging to them.

In 1898 a joint high commission was established to reach a compromise. The U.S. abandoned the agreement when U.S. domestic politics interfered. When Teddy Roosevelt won the presidency he applied his motto, "speak softly and carry a big stick" toward the dispute. Canadians were harassed in several ways.

Finally in 1903 the Hay/Herbert Treaty was established. It called for a six member tribunal made up of three Americans, two Canadians and one British member, to make a decision. Guess who won?

After the First World War began, and Canada sent an expeditionary force to France, the U.S. was content to remain on the sidelines and simply supply Britain with armaments until they had drained the U.K. of its American assets. After the U.S. entered the war in 1917 it did play a decisive role but did not fight the war single-handed as some U.S. history books imply. Many Americans would be surprised to learn that Canada suffered about half as many casualties in that war as the United States despite them being ten times our size.

Of their several plans for conquering Canada the one that is least known, and by far the most shocking, is Joint Plan Red. Prepared by the old Joint Board of the Army and Navy, precursor of the Chiefs of Staff Committee, and approved by the secretaries of war and the navy in May 1930, Joint Plan Red posed a threat graver than the coming depression: war with the British Empire.

The essence of the plan was to concentrate U.S. naval power in the Atlantic before the British were aware and then launch lightning attacks on Montreal and Halifax in order to prevent reinforcements from arriving from the U.K.

As preposterous as such a plan appears in retrospect, and prepared just 12 years after U.S. troops had fought side-by-side with British and Canadian troops in France, it nevertheless is a fact. One of the reasons for the plan was to tip the balance in favour of U.S. commercial interests. It is convenient to explain Joint Plan Red now as "just an exercise" but that is hard to credit. It was, until it was declassified in February 1974, one of America's most tightly guarded military secrets.[19]

Once again in 1939 the U.S. was not prepared to go to war on behalf of freedom. True, some Americans joined the Canadian Forces but it was not until the Japanese attacked Pearl Harbor on December 7, 1941, that President Franklin D. Roosevelt was able to get Congressional approval for a declaration of war.

Military historians point out that since the Ogdensburg Agreement of 1940 there has been a close military cooperation between the U.S. and Canada in the joint defence of North America. This partnership, established to meet the needs of World War II, was subsequently extended to the Cold War period through cooperation in both the North Atlantic Treaty Organization and the North American Air (later Aerospace) Defense Command at Colorado Springs.

People on both sides of the border who claim that the U.S. carried the major burden of the Cold War years are quite correct. To extend that argument to the point where it is portrayed as U.S. concern for the defence of Canada, however, is true only in the most technical sense. The U.S.

was concerned about the protection of its own territory and Canada's inclusion was incidental to that end. Their interest might well be called a "collateral benefit" for us.

With the end of the Cold War, however, times have changed. Neither Canada nor the U.S. are threatened militarily from outside. Canada, however, has new concerns that are closer to home. With the signature of the Free Trade Agreement, in 1988, U.S. strategy toward Canada took on an entirely new focus. President Ronald Reagan managed to accomplish with one stroke of a pen what U.S. armies had failed to do on several occasions. He conquered Canada – at least *pro tem*.

This is not a new idea as any casual reading of history will attest. For more than half a century we have been included in what the U.S. Council on Foreign Relations called the Grand Area but which is now being updated to something more relevant to the times, "The Project for a New American Century," which is a pseudonym for The New American Empire.

If this were not worrisome enough, part of the mandate of the men dedicated to building the empire is the belief that because the U.S. has been so richly blessed it has a God-given Imperial mandate to impose its values and interests on the world at large. That worries me a lot.

CHAPTER 3

AMERICAN VALUES AND INTERESTS

"Power corrupts and absolute power corrupts absolutely."

Lord Acton

I have sometimes written about the best of American values and traits. Their universities are among the finest in the world. Their museums and art galleries are world class. Their scientists are usually on the cutting edge. Their technology is unsurpassed. Their ingenuity and productivity are legend. And the American dream of becoming a self-made millionaire or billionaire lives on.

These characteristics are to be admired and can be copied or adapted by anyone wishing to replicate, even in some small way, their many achievements. But there is a dark side to America as well. The greed and self-centredness of its leaders; its false gods; its double standards; its increasing disparity of income between rich and poor; its callous attitude toward the poor and the powerless.

It is these latter traits which we should be fearful of in a world dominated by the United States. The motivation of its leaders appears to be increasingly incompatible with life, liberty and the pursuit of happiness either in the U.S. itself or in those vast areas of the world it seeks to dominate. The game plan is not to provide the bread of life to starving millions but to exploit and manipulate the many for the benefit of the elite few.

To see the picture more clearly it is very important to understand who is really running the United States and the methods used to achieve and maintain their power. Is there a long stretch between rhetoric and reality when it comes to liberty, democracy and the rule of law?

THE PERMANENT GOVERNMENT

Lewis Lapham, editor of *Harper's* magazine and one of America's great liberal thinkers, contends that the United States has two governments – "permanent" and "provisional." He summed up his definition of the former in one sentence as part of his 'On Politics, Culture and the Media' keynote address to the Canadian Institute of International Affairs national foreign policy conference in October, 1996. "The permanent government is the secular oligarchy that comprises the *Fortune 500*, the big media and entertainment syndicates, the civil and military services, the large research universities and law firms."[1]

That pretty well sums it up. Professional lobbyists, all too often former senior government officials; public relations firms and lawyers; the international banks with their close ties to both the Federal Reserve and the Treasury Department, not to mention the International Monetary Fund and the World Bank; the close almost incestuous relationship between Bretton Woods institutions and the State and Treasury Departments; the information conglomerates that blur the lines between news, culture and flag-waving; these are all parts of the permanent government that holds the reins of real power.

Lapham puts it in historical context. "Just as the Catholic Church was the predominant institution in medieval Europe, and the Roman Legion the most efficient manifestation of organized force in the 1st and 2nd centuries BC, so also the transnational corporation arranges the affairs of the late 20th [and early 21st] century. The American Congress and the American President serve at the pleasure of their commercial overlords, all of whom hold firmly to the belief that all government regulation is wicked (that is, the work of the Devil) and that any impulse that runs counter to the manly interests of business is, by definition, soft, effeminate and liberal."[2]

Many members of the permanent government have banded together in organizations for purposes of discussion, communication and planning – including plans for the world without economic borders, sometimes referred to as the New World Order. The three most important groups are The Council on Foreign Relations; the Bilderbergers, of European origin, but with many important North American members; and the Trilateral Commission.

The Council on Foreign Relations (CFR or Council) is the oldest of the three. Although it was active in the 1920s and 1930s it only came into a position of great influence with the outbreak of World War II. As early as October, 1940, its Economic and Financial Group drafted a memorandum outlining a comprehensive policy, "... to set forth the political, military, territorial and economic requirements of the United States in its potential leadership of the non-German world area including the United Kingdom itself as well as the Western hemisphere and Far East."[3]

The "Grand Area," as the non-German bloc was called in 1941, was insufficiently grand. The preferred ideal was all-inclusive – one world economy dominated by the United States. It was at this stage that there was a virtual merger of the Council and the U.S. State Department which, in late 1941, created a special commission to consider positive planning. The Advisory Committee on Positive Foreign Policy, on which Council members played important roles, set the stage for key decisions that would affect the post-war world.

The Council influenced plans for international economic institutions including the International Monetary Fund (IMF) and the International Bank for Reconstruction and Development (World Bank). It was also deeply involved in the creation of the United Nations. At a meeting in May, 1942, one of the Council members, Isaiah Bowman, argued that the United States had to exercise the strength to assure "security," and at the same time "avoid conventional forms of imperialism." The way to do this, he suggested, was to make the exercise of that power international in character through a United Nations body.[4]

It was clear at all times that the purpose of the Grand Area and, later, world hegemony was to support an expanding U.S. economy – to provide it with raw materials and markets for its products. This was labelled the "national interest." It was equally clear that the "national interest" was the interest of the ruling elite whose members comprised the Council. The real interests of the majority of rank-and-file Americans were never a factor in the equation.

The Bilderbergers, who got their name from the group's first meeting place at the Hotel de Bilderberg of Oosterbeek, Holland,[5] is a highly secretive organization which influences policy through the good auspices of individual members in many countries, including the United States. Some of these individuals are prominent in the CFR and the Trilateral Commission, which is the most open of the three as well as being the one which is politically proactive.

The Trilateral Commission is the youngest of the three major groups having been founded in 1973 under the auspices of Zbigniew Brzezinski, then a Columbia University professor, and David Rockefeller, who was already a powerful member of the other two groups. Of the three, the Trilats, as I call them, are the most open about their aims and objectives. They are also elitist and anti-democratic.

A 1975 report entitled "The Crisis of Democracy: Report on the Governability of Democracies to the Trilateral Commission," states: "The vulnerability of democratic government in the United States comes not primarily from external threats, though such threats are real, not from internal subversion from the left or right, although both possibilities could exist, but rather from internal dynamics of democracy itself in a highly educated, mobilized, and participant society."[6] Wow, the principal danger to democratic governments is democracy. That is a concept that you have to dig deep to come up with. What about the danger to democracy of actions taken by governments "elected" by the people, but only after being chosen and "installed" in positions of leadership by elite groups like the Trilateral Commission?

THE "PROVISIONAL" GOVERNMENT

The Trilats have picked and elected every U.S. president except one beginning with Jimmy Carter, a member of the Commission.   When they became somewhat disillusioned with him they decided to replace him with another one of their own, George Bush.[7] A small problem arose when Bush ran for the Republican nomination. Opponents in five states ran full page ads saying, "The same people who gave you Jimmy Carter are giving you George Bush."

When Bush couldn't win the primary, the Trilats had to settle for a Reagan-Bush ticket and Bush had to bide his time while Reagan, who had been looked on with some skepticism, really came through for them. He not only increased defence spending dramatically, and promised the development of a "Star Wars" capability, he really delivered for them with the successful negotiations of the Canada-U.S. Free Trade Agreement.

The whole election process has become a charade. The permanent government picks the actors to go on stage and read the scripts written by themselves. Applicants are carefully screened in advance in the hope of finding candidates who will stick to their scripts and not be prone to major improvization once they get on stage.

The thought ran through my head as I watched George W. Bush read his carefully prepared foreign policy in a telecast before the 2000 presidential election. He was all for expanding free trade and promoting the New World Order.

The permanent government will like that, I said to myself. Indeed they did. He was their boy. Why did he win the Idaho straw vote which was a critical step toward winning the Republican primary? Because he spent the most money. And why could be spend the most money? Because the Trilats had picked him ahead of other Republican hopefuls to be their standard bearer.

By the time the campaign of 2000 was over the amount of money that had been raised and spent on behalf of George W. Bush, was little short of astronomical. Total receipts, including federal funds of $67,560,000, were $193,088,650 of which only $185,921,855 was spent leaving a surplus of $7,201,734 cash on hand. The candidate himself was not required to put up any cash.[8]

In the majority of cases, thought not all, the source of the private funds was disclosed. Just over $75 million was totally transparent, about half a million partially so, and the balance of just over $10 million included no information about the donor's employer and/or occupation.[9]

The top contributors:[10]

MBNA Corp.	$240,675
Vinson & Elkins	$202,850
Credit Suisse First Boston	$191,400
Ernst & Young	$179,949
Andersen Worldwide	$145,650
Morgan Stanley Dean Witter & Co.	$144,900
Merrill Lynch	$132,425
PriceWaterhouseCoopers	$127,798
Baker & Botts	$116,121
Citigroup Inc.	$114,300
Goldman Sachs Group	$113,999
Enron Corp.	$113,800
Bank of America	$112,500
KPMG LLP	$107,744
Jenkens & Gilchrist	$105,450
Enterprise Rent-A-Car	$ 97,498
State of Texas	$ 87,254
American General Corp.	$ 84,134
Deloitte & Touche	$ 81,600
AXA Financial	$ 79,725

It is patently obvious that an electoral system requiring such vast sums of private money to guarantee success is not really democracy. It is government by the rich minority for the benefit of the rich minority – a plutocracy of the elite. This is the system the U.S. administration wishes to impose on the world at large because every replica, whether in Canada, Russia or Iraq, becomes a conduit for benefits to flow to the top of the pyramid.

One has to wonder what kind of people really run America and, by extension, the world. What are they like?

MANY ARE GREEDY BEES

Greed is one of the defining characteristics of many of the people, mostly men, who run America. Like bees, they address one flower after another in order to slurp up their nectar. And when they run out of flowers within their borders they connive to erase the border and gain access to other peoples' gardens and meadows.

Executive compensation provides an almost infallible yardstick of greed. Just take a look at the following list rounded down to the nearest million. Jeffrey C. Barbakow, Tenet Healthcare, $116 million; Dwight C. Schar, NVR, $94 million; Michael S. Dell, Dell Computer, $82 million; Irwin M. Jacobs, Qualcomm, $63 million; Barry Diller, USA Interactive, $53 million; Dan M. Palmer, Concord EFS, $43 million; Charles T. Fote, First Data, $39 million; Orin C. Smith, Starbucks, $38 million; Richard S. Fuld Jr., Lehman Bros. Holdings, $29 million; Maurice R. Greenberg, Intl. Group, $29 million; and 15 others with total compensation packages of $19 million or more.[11]

This is obscene! I have never met a man who I thought was worth more than a million a year. Oh I am well aware that a technical case can be made. A new CEO takes over an ailing company, fires a few thousand people, overworks those who remain, reduces costs, increases profits and claims a generous slice of the benefit. A small bonus would be in order, but not wholesale robbery!

Furthermore, the *Forbes* magazine list of corporate compensation indicates that the bloated packages were paid to executives with efficiency grades ranging from A to F. So it appears that once the bad habit is acquired it becomes an addiction.

This trend is extremely worrisome. When Peter G. Peterson, Chairman of the Council on Foreign Relations, came to Canada in the fall of 2002 as part of a worldwide campaign to get people to understand U.S. foreign policy better, he agreed to take questions at the end of his address jointly sponsored by the Canadian Institute of International Affairs and the Ramsay Luncheon Series. In response to one on the subject of corporate governance he was merciless. Ten years ago the average CEO's salary was 40 times the average of his employees. Now it is 400 times the average of subordinates.[12] Is there any stronger word than greed?

It would be quite unfair to suggest that only U.S. executives are greedy bees. But it is fair to say that the trend toward excessive compensation began in the U.S. and then spread north into Canada and across the ocean to Europe. But that is the root of the problem. We are talking about U.S. hegemony and the determined effort to impose American "values" on a skeptical world.

SOME OF THE ELITE CUT CORNERS

Cutting corners is as old as the world itself but some recent cases appear to establish new benchmarks for the magnitude of deceit. The collapse of Enron Corp. is now a textbook example. It would be redundant to repeat the story here except to say that the collapse revealed that the books had been deliberately and methodically falsified. Worse, this was done with the knowledge and cooperation of some of its auditors.

There was even a Canadian connection. According to a 218-page report by a special committee of Enron's board of directors, the company took a $110 million (U.S.) loan from the Canadian Imperial Bank of Commerce and booked it as a profit. "This is a devastating report. ... It suggests massive problems. This is almost a culture of corruption here," U.S. Congressman Byron Dorgan said on NBC's "Meet the Press." "One billion in profit was booked here that didn't exist. That's trouble."[13]

As a footnote to history, Kenneth Lay, president of Enron Corp. when it collapsed, was a director of the right-wing American Enterprise Institute. He was also a member of the Trilateral Commission and was selected to receive the Private Sector Council's 1997 Leadership Award, received the 1998 Horatio Alger Award and was named by *Business Week* as one of the top 25 managers in the world for 1999. Mr. Lay is a member of the Texas Business Hall of Fame. A friend of President George W. Bush, Mr. Lay's Enron contributed $113,800 to his 2000 campaign fund.

Not to be outdone, WorldCom topped them all in order of magnitude – the largest Chapter 11 bankruptcy ever filed in the United States. In May 2003, MCI, the former WorldCom, agreed to settle accusations of fraud by the Securities and Exchange Commission by paying a $500 million penalty that will ultimately be given to investors.[14]

Lawyers representing investors, led by the New York State employees' pension fund, who have filed a class-action lawsuit said that the $500 million would not satisfy claims of shareholders who say they have lost "tens of billions of dollars" from MCI's misleading accounting.[15]

These major scandals arising from greed extending into fraud have attracted the most public attention and comment. They provided grist for the cocktail circuit mill for months. Many executive reputations were ruined, some charges were laid, investors lost their savings while employees lost their jobs and pensions. But in a way they were only the tip of a much more ominous iceberg – widespread cheating by many of the most prestigious firms on Wall Street.

The list is a who's who of world finance. Salomon; Merrill; Credit Suisse Group's CSFB; Morgan Stanley; Goldman Sachs; Bear Stearns; J.P. Morgan Chase; Lehman Brothers; U.S. Bancorp. At firm after firm, according to prosecutors, analysts wittingly duped investors to curry favour with corporate clients. Investment houses received secret payments from companies they gave strong recommendations to buy. And for top executives whose companies were clients, stock underwriters offered special access to hot initial public offerings, the *New York Times* opined.[16]

Brian Miller, writing in the *Globe and Mail*, said: "There's little repentance on Wall Street these days. Even after 10 major securities firms agreed to pay a combined $1.4 billion (U.S.) in penalties and costs to put the scandal behind them – a tiny fraction of their profits during that era – not one has admitted any wrongdoing and probably never will."[17]

The Wall Street honchos' notion that investors have only themselves to blame is disingenuous to say the least. They invested, in many cases, on the basis of dishonest information. When Philip Purcell, chief executive of Morgan Stanley, insisted there was nothing improper about revelations that his firm and others had paid one another to issue bullish research reports on their investment banking clients, he was kidding no one but himself.[18] What he was describing was fraudulent behaviour.

Further, his company was one of the worst offenders. It used four ratings for stocks: 'strong buy,' 'outperform,' 'neutral' and 'underperform.' Four of its leading analysts continued to maintain 'outperform' ratings on at least 13 stocks even as they declined in value by 74 to 96 percent.[19] Little wonder that David Wessel wrote in the *Globe and Mail*: "The scope and scale of the corporate transgressions of the late 1990s, now coming to light, exceed anything the U.S. has witnessed since the years preceding the Great Depression."[20]

Once again, I am sad to say, the transgressions are not exclusive to the United States. But once again I have to ask if we are obliged to adopt American "values" as our own?

Leonard Brooks, a professor of business ethics at the University of Toronto, traces many recent problems to a cultural shift in the Canadian establishment. "Even a decade ago, he says, Bay Street prided itself on prudence and conservatism. But with North American markets becoming much more tightly entwined, many Canadian companies have thrown off the traditional drab mantle and searched out chief executives fashioned in the mode of swashbuckling corporate raiders and daring visionaries embraced by Wall Street."[21]

Generalizations are always odious but one cannot escape the conclusion that many of the key people in the pyramid of power have abandoned those values on which the Republic was founded. Our American cousins have lost their moral compass and it is my fear that we Canadians will meekly follow along in their path for want of a moral compass of our own.

CHAPTER 4

A COMPASS IN NEED OF REPAIR

"I repeat... that all power is a trust – that we are accountable for its exercise – that, from the people, and for the people, all springs, and all must exist"

Benjamin Disraeli

Anyone who really cares about the United States has to be concerned about what has gone wrong in the great Republic. Have constitutional rights been abrogated without due process? What has happened to the rule of law, the freedom of speech and assembly, to equality under the law, to the distribution of income, to the provision of health care, to transparency in awarding contracts and to priorities in public spending?

There are many thoughtful Americans who are asking these sorts of questions. Congressman Dennis J. Kucinich raised several in "A Prayer for America," a speech to the Southern California Americans for Democratic Action in Los Angeles.

"Let us pray that our nation will remember that the unfolding of the promise of democracy in our nation paralleled the striving for civil rights. That is why we must challenge the rationale of the Patriot Act. We must ask why should America put aside guarantees of constitutional justice?

"How can we justify in effect canceling the First Amendment and the right of free speech, the right to peaceable assembly?

"How can we justify in effect canceling the Fourth Amendment, probable cause, the prohibitions against unreasonable search and seizure?

"How can we justify in effect canceling the Fifth Amendment, nullifying due process, and allowing for indefinite incarceration without a trial?

"How can we justify in effect canceling the Sixth Amendment, the right to prompt and public trial?

"How can we justify in effect canceling the Eighth Amendment which protects against cruel and unusual punishment?

"We cannot justify widespread wiretaps and internet surveillance without judicial supervision, let alone with it.

"We cannot justify secret searches without a warrant.

"We cannot justify giving the Attorney General the ability to designate domestic terror groups.

"We cannot justify giving the FBI total access to any type of data which may exist in any system anywhere such as medical records and financial records.

"We cannot justify giving the CIA the ability to target people in this country for intelligence surveillance.

"We cannot justify a government which takes from the people our right to privacy and then assumes for its own operations a right to total secrecy."[1]

All of this in a country where the president, on first taking office, is required to take the following oath.

"I do solemnly swear (or affirm) that I will faithfully execute the office of President of the United States, and will to the best of my ability, preserve, protect, and defend the Constitution of the United States."[2]

There appears to be a very wide gulf between the theory and the practice. As Congressman Kucinich pointed out, several key sections of the U.S. Constitution have been arbitrarily suspended. Is it consistent with American "values" to have FBI agents visiting places of worship? And if only mosques were targeted, is this upholding the constitutional guarantee of equality under the law? It is good to recall that freedom of worship was one of the cornerstones of the Republic.

Then there is the question of holding people in detention indefinitely without charges being laid in clear violation of the Fifth Amendment.   The Justice Department report to Congress states that "fewer than 50" people were held as material witnesses in connection with the September 11th attacks,[3] but does the Constitution set numerical exceptions to the important principles it enshrines?

All Americans of good conscience should be outraged by the Pentagon's plans for an antiterrorism surveillance system. "The program, known as Terrorist Information Awareness – a change from the original, more Orwellian name, Total Information Awareness – calls for creating a huge computer database to track individuals.   It is directed by retired Admiral John Poindexter, whose misjudgments as Ronald Reagan's national security adviser helped produce the Iran-contra affair."[4]

Talk about un-American activity, this proposal rates star billing.   Why is all this information required?   To what purpose will it be put?   And if there is a legitimate reason, which I profoundly doubt, why isn't it being administered by the Justice Department rather than the Pentagon?   There is something profoundly disturbing about hot warriors meddling in the administration of justice.

Canadians, too, should be worried about the Total Information Awareness program.   A massive amount of our data is processed in the United States and will all come under the watchful eye of "big uncle."   Canadian privacy laws will not protect us.   And this is particularly disconcerting in the longer range if the Pentagon is allowed to continue with the development and installation of space weapons that will be capable of zapping any individual person on earth within a radius of one metre.

ILLEGAL COMBATANTS

The case of the illegal combatants is one of the most morally distressing on the world agenda.   There are the 600 or so detainees from 43 countries being held at the Guantanamo Bay Naval Base located on a 45-square-mile area near Cuba's eastern tip.   The land was seized by the

United States in the Spanish-American War and held under a 1903 lease from Cuba.

Who is an illegal combatant? Anyone under the physical control of the Pentagon who is designated as such. Where did the term come from? It was manufactured by the Pentagon as a device for evading both U.S. national and international law. The designation means that the men are neither under a civilian indictment – meaning they would have access to counsel – or prisoners of war, who could not be interrogated and would have to be released at the end of hostilities.

Instead, the men who have been denied access to both their families and legal counsel, will be tried by military tribunals. If U.S. plans to turn Guantanamo Bay into a death camp, with its own death row and execution chambers are implemented, prisoners could be "tried, convicted and executed without leavings its boundaries, without a jury and without right of appeal."[5]

American law professor Jonathan Turley, who has led U.S. civil rights group protests against the plan to have military tribunals to hear cases at Guantanamo Bay, said: "It is not surprising the authorities are building a death row because they have said they plan to try capital cases before these tribunals. This camp was created to execute people. The administration has no interest in long-term prison sentences for people it regards as hard-core terrorists."[6]

If the U.S. does execute al-Qaeda and Taliban prisoners at Guantanamo it will fly in the face of public opinion in Great Britain, Canada and many other parts of the civilized world which increasingly regard the practice of capital punishment as barbaric. They will also be overlooking the lesson which can be drawn from Israel's experience with the Palestinians. Killing an alleged terrorist may only result in the birth of two more.

For the U.S. to understand how the world regards their actions they should use insight to imagine how they would feel if the shoe were on the other foot. Assume that some foreign power captured a number of CIA agents, designated them as illegal combatants and took them to a remote island.

Once there they were denied access to families and counsel before being tried, convicted and executed for alleged capital crimes they had committed.   Does anyone possess an imagination wild enough to predict what the reaction of the United States might be?

FREEDOM OF EXPRESSION

It is an old axiom that the first casualty of war is truth. That is taken as a given.   Now we have to extend the definition to include reasons given for launching a war – especially a preventive war of doubtful validity.   President Bush solemnly stated that the war in Iraq was essential because that country possessed weapons of mass destruction that posed a clear and imminent threat to the United States.

As I said earlier, the message was repeated so often that the vast majority of people in the English-speaking world believed it – most of those who read our right-wing newspapers and watch CNN.   The brainwashing was less effective in countries that get their news in languages other than English – the Russians, Chinese, the Germans and the French – especially the French, who were totally reviled.

Their sin, of course, was to understand what was really going on before anyone admitted it.   They refused to be kicked around by a super-power about to launch a war in aid of its own strategic interests.   Standing on what they considered to be an important point of principle cost the French dearly – seeing their wine poured down gutters and, in one act of incredible silliness, having the word French removed from French fries on the menu of the Congressional restaurant.

So there must have been a few knowing smiles along the Champs-Elysées when Paul Wolfowitz, Deputy Defense Secretary and a principal architect of the war on Iraq, admitted that finding banned weapons was never Washington's only reason for invading Iraq.   "For bureaucratic reasons, we settled on one issue, weapons of mass destruction, because it was the one reason everyone would agree on," Mr. Wolfowitz told *Vanity Fair* magazine.[7]

He said a less public, but important reason for invading Iraq was to allow the Pentagon to remove U.S. troops protecting Saudi Arabia. Their presence had been fueling tension with Islamic fundamentalists in the kingdom and providing ammunition for al-Qaeda's terrorist campaign.[8] This revelation raises serious questions about the truthfulness of the Pentagon's assertion that it does not plan to maintain permanent military bases in Iraq.

In this scenario of grand deception on the part of the White House and the Pentagon the importance of upholding the First Amendment, including the right of free speech and dissent, is paramount. The press has been far too deferential and there have been far too many cases of bitter consequences for people who exercised what they thought was a fundamental right in America.

One example involved Bill Maher, a man who "makes his living being controversial and politically incorrect. Maher made the observation that firing a rocket from a submarine on a target a thousand miles or so away did not strike him as a courageous act. He went on to say – pressing his luck – that whatever else could be said about terrorist suicide bombers, one could not call them cowards."[9]

His statement resulted in an explosion of angered outrage, as well as the cancellation of Maher's show by a number of right-thinking, patriotic television and cable executives. All this furor in retribution for exercising the kind of fundamental right for which men and women have fought and died to maintain. Not only that, but for stating what some impartial observers might consider an undeniable truth.

Nashville roots rocker Steve Earle stirred up a storm when he opted for the politically incorrect. Hence the vilification he endured over his song about American Taliban fighter John Walker Lindh. The right-wing outcry against "John Walker Blues" is still reverberating across the mountain tops.

"Even more disturbing than his own travails," says Earle, "is the campaign against the Dixie Chicks. The popular trio faced a boycott by broadcast and concert promotion giant Clear-Channel after one of its members, Natalie Maines, made a disparaging remark about President Bush."[10] Natalie was imprudent enough to say that she was ashamed that President Bush came from Texas.

Well, well. No doubt there are a handful of people in Texas who agree with her as compared to the vast majority who are proud to have their boy in the White House, and might be tempted to dub him Saint George in deference to his piety. But that isn't the point. As Earle says, artists ought to be able to say what they want to say. That's why they're artists.

"In Earle's view, the Patriot Act, a bundle of security measures instituted after the terrorist attacks of September 11, 2001, is the most serious breach of individual freedoms in the U.S. since the anti-communist witch hunt of the 1950s. And, he adds, the unwillingness of opposition Democrats to be cast as unpatriotic has made it even more impossible for artists to speak out ... Other artists, he contends, are holding their tongues for fear of being blacklisted."[11]

Is living in fear of arbitrary arrest, or being blacklisted for speaking your mind consistent with the "freedom" Americans trumpet to the world?

"We will defend freedom at any cost," President Bush declared to applause from workers at a family-owned Iowa printing company in response to opposition questions about the cost and aims of the war against terrorism.[12] One has to wonder if there are any qualifications such as the colour of your skin, your religion, or the political correctness of your opinions.

THE DOUBLE STANDARD

Although it is fair to say that all of us as individuals, and all nation states, frequently employ double standards in decision making, it is certainly fair to say that the United States is not immune to the practice. It is the extent to which a person or country strives to resist the temptation to treat some people or classes of people or nations less beneficially than others that provides one useful yardstick of ethical behaviour.

One of the most blatant examples of recent memory has been in the punishment meted out to various classes of cheaters. Specifically, the relative treatment of some of the richest, most powerful men on Wall Street compared to that of some petty thieves. As I pointed out earlier, ten of the Street's most prominent firms agreed to a $1.4 billion settlement for indulging in practices that pumped up stock prices before they collapsed and more than $7 trillion in shareholder value went up in smoke.

William Donaldson, chairman of the U.S. Securities and Exchange Commission lauded the agreement and called it "an important new chapter in our ongoing efforts to restore investors' faith and confidence in the fairness and integrity of our markets."[13] I wish that I shared his confidence but I don't. There are myriad previous examples of Wall Street firms ripping off the public. There have been other settlements. There has seldom, if ever, been contrition.

At the time of writing there is news of ongoing criminal investigations of some of the senior and chief executive officers to determine their knowledge of and possible complicity in the wholesale fraud of unsuspecting investors. If history repeats itself, the odds are that none of the world's most notorious "unarmed robbers" will go to jail. Instead they will get off with their tiny fines which basically sanction the status quo.

Contrast this with the penalties applied to two shoplifters under California's "three strikes" law. They may receive sentences up to life in prison without violating constitutional safeguards under cruel and unusual punishment. "In two major 5 to 4 decisions in March, 2003, the U.S. Supreme Court upheld the lengthy prison sentences of two California shoplifters, saying that three-strikes laws are a valid means for state lawmakers and voters to attempt to sweep career criminals off the streets – even when their third crime is a relatively minor one."[14]

It is true that the sentence isn't just for that crime. Leondro Andrade, who was caught shoplifting $153 worth of children's videos, was a heroin addict with prior convictions for marijuana trafficking, prison escape, burglary and petty theft. It was the shoplifting offence, however, for which he was sentenced to 50 years to life without eligibility for parole until he is 87 years of age.

In the other case, Gary Ewing, who was sentenced to 25 years in prison for attempting to shoplift three golf clubs from a pro shop by stuffing the clubs down his pant leg, had several prior convictions for residential burglary and robbery armed with a knife. Ewing, who was on parole at the time of the shoplifting attempt, won't be eligible for parole again until he is 63. The high court affirmed the sentence meted out and upheld by California state judges.

In the Andrade case, the court revised a ruling by a three-judge panel of the Ninth U.S. Circuit Court of Appeal. The appeals court had ruled 2 to 1 that Andrade's sentence was grossly disproportionate and thus violated Eighth Amendment protection. Four of the nine high court justices must have shared that view.

"In a dissent joined by three other justices, Justice David Souter said there was no justifiable reason for such long sentences. 'Whether or not one accepts the state's choice of penalogical policy as constitutionally sound, that policy cannot reasonably justify the imposition of a consecutive 25-year minimum for a second minor offence committed soon after the first triggering offense,' he said."[15]

There is an old adage which says, "Let the punishment fit the crime." If this kind of justice could be applied literally, the shoplifters could satisfy their debt to society with very short terms while a number of Wall Street tycoons would be obliged to feast on prison fare for the rest of their natural days.

HEALTH CARE

In few areas of American policy is the double standard as starkly pronounced as in health care. For the rich, the U.S. unquestionably provides the best health care of any country in the world. The poor, however, do not fare equally. Millions of Americans run the risk of financial disaster in the event of serious illness.

A recent study by the Congressional Budget Office indicated that nearly 60 million Americans lack health insurance at some point in the year. The report said 57 million to 59 million people, "about a quarter of the non-elderly population," lacked insurance at some time in 1998, the most recent year for which reliable comparative figures were available.[16]

At the same time the report indicated that the commonly used Census Bureau figures of 41 million people without health care is high when applied to the entire year. The budget office referred to government surveys suggesting that the number of people uninsured for the entire year was 21 to 31 million, or 9 to 13 percent of non-elderly Americans.[17]

So for millions of Americans their problem can be solved by getting sick during that part of the year when they are insured. Actually this is no laughing matter. A Washington D.C. couple, who had been dear friends of mine for many years, saw disaster strike unexpectedly. The husband, who had never been sick a day in his life, arrived home from a trip feeling tired and ill. By the time he died, 65 days later, he had run up medical and hospital bills in the amount of $215,000.[18] This is not a sad story from some third world country. Its locale was the capital of the richest most powerful country on earth.

Even millions of people who are insured risk losing it or having benefits sharply curtailed by cash-starved states. State officials, wrestling with their third year of fiscal crisis say they have no choice but to rein in Medicaid, the fast-growing program that provides health insurance for 50 million people.

"Many state officials are pleading for federal help as they face an array of painful trade-offs, often pitting the needs of impoverished elderly people for prescription drugs and long-term care, against those of low-income families seeking basic health coverage."[19]

Meanwhile the perennial debate between supporters of state-sponsored health care and those who favour private providers rages on. Republicans in Congress, in the spring of 2003, indicated they had accepted President Bush's proposal to encourage the development of private health plans. At the same time these efforts to revamp Medicare "have been immensely complicated by new data suggesting that such plans would not save money and could substantially increase Medicare costs."[20]

Another shadow was cast over the industry when Richard M. Scrushy, co-founder of HealthSouth Corp. of Birmingham, Alabama, the largest U.S. operator of rehabilitation hospitals and clinics, with about 1,700 health care centres, 51,000 employees and $4.3 billion in 2002 revenues, was fired.

In March, 2003, Scrushy and HealthSouth were accused by the U.S. Securities and Exchange Commission of overstating company profits by at least $1.4 billion over the past four years. Scrushy, one of the most dynamic promoters of private hospitals, fought to lift a court-imposed freeze on his personal assets claiming that, "he needs $60 million (U.S.) for annual living expenses, and another $60 million to cover legal expenses."[21]

TAX BREAKS

President Bush appeared to be so anxious to get his tax relief bill adopted by Congress before Memorial Day 2003 that he was willing to accept a grab bag that included some of his own proposals, bundled in some candy wrapping like child-care credits and relief for married taxpayers. Cynics will be quick to point out that the latter are subject to a "sunset" expiry after three years in order to fudge the magnitude of the whole deal.

The economic wisdom of the proposal was dubious from the outset. As the *New York Times* pointed out in an editorial on May 22, 2003, the package "again offers the most significant relief to the upper-bracket Americans so dear to the administration."[22] If the idea was to stimulate the economy, as advertised, that is the least effective way to go about it. By what magic does stimulation of the stock market translate into jobs and significant growth in the real economy?

The new tax scales do not address the double standard involved in a worsening economic equality. According to the

U.S. Census Bureau, the bottom 40 percent of American families earned 18 percent of the national income in 1970, but by 1998 they earned only 14 percent – and that figure could fall to 10 percent before too long.[23]

Robert J. Shiller, professor of economics at Yale and author of *The New Financial Order: Risk in the 21st Century*, in an article in the *New York Times* suggested that the "basic framework for tax law doesn't make much sense. Instead future tax brackets and rates should be contingent on the extent of future inequality."[24]

He goes on to underline the urgency of such a reform. "When the top tenth of the population has attained such a high percentage of society's wealth that it can effectively block any reform, it can be counted on to use its power to keep its riches. America ought to act now to make sure this never comes to pass."[25]

Unfortunately, I think that point has already been reached and that the rich are already firmly in control. The only evidence that would convince me otherwise would be a reversal of the trend and an actual closing of the income gap.

TRANSPARENCY

There are many other areas where the double standard applies but there is little point in mentioning them. So my last example will be a very brief reference to the question of transparency about which far too much is said, and far too little done to lift the veil of secrecy. The double standard is that governments want to know more and more about us while wanting us to know less and less of what they are up to.

The new data bank to be compiled by the Pentagon is a case in point. The whole idea is enough to scare the bejeebers out of anyone who values his or her privacy. The idea is especially worrisome to anyone who has ever had any experience with credit bureaus and witnessed the errors and cases of mistaken identity. This is a hundred times more serious as we embark on a new era when the English common law is turned on its end and instead of being presumed innocent until proven guilty, one is assumed to be guilty unless and until innocence can be proven.

Contrast this with the tendency for governments to let important contracts without calling for tenders and for keeping the details secret until someone is persistent enough to dig for them. The emergency contract the Bush Administration gave to Halliburton to extinguish Iraqi oil fires is a fine example. An emergency fire-fighting contract might or might not have been justified; but should it be used as a cover for a much longer and more lucrative role in helping repair Iraq's oil system?

This company, once run by Vice-President Dick Cheney, has a checkered past which has been monitored by Democratic Congressman Henry Waxman of California, who deserves credit for exposing the extent of the questionable contract. "Only now, over five weeks after the contract was first disclosed, are members of Congress and the public learning that Halliburton may be asked to pump and distribute Iraqi oil under contract," Waxman said on May 6, 2003.[26] The Congressman repeated the Army Corps of Engineers statement that the contract could be worth up to $7 billion for two years but that figure was a cap based on a worst-case event of oil well fires.[27]

Congressman Waxman has raised pointed questions about this company which is considered a court favourite even though it has made a lot of money doing business in countries that sponsor terrorism, including members of the Axis of Evil that is so despised by the President. In an April 30, 2003 letter to Defense Secretary Donald Rumsfeld, he wrote:

"Since at least the 1980s, federal laws have prohibited U.S. companies from doing business in one or more of these countries. Yet Halliburton appears to have sought to circumvent these restrictions by setting up subsidiaries in foreign countries and territories such as the Cayman Islands. These actions started as early as 1984; they appear to have continued during the period between 1995 and 2000, when Vice President Cheney headed the company; and they are apparently ongoing even today."[28]

Mr. Waxman said a subsidiary called Halliburton Products and Services opened an office in Tehran, Iran, in February 2000 to undertake offshore drilling projects, while asserting, "we are committed to position ourselves in a market that offers huge growth potential." Now, with the U.S. takeover of Iraq, Halliburton, through its subsidiary, Kellogg Brown & Root has hit the jackpot by being given control of the Iraqi oil operations, including oil distribution. Mr. Waxman noted that the long-term contract was at odds with administration statements that Iraq's oil belongs to the Iraqi people.[29]

The double standard appears to apply equally to the question of transparency and the dubious practice of rewarding countries that defy U.S. law and consort with the alleged "enemy." The moral compass needs more than fine tuning. It needs a complete overhaul. Meanwhile it is responsible for national and spending priorities that are badly skewed.

CHAPTER 5

LEADERSHIP LOST

"Every gun that is made, every warship launched, every rocket fired signifies, in a final scene, a theft from those who hunger and are not fed, those who are cold and are not clothed. This world in arms is not spending money alone. It is spending the sweat of its laborers, the genius of its scientists, the hopes of its children."

Dwight D. Eisenhower

The most dramatic demonstration of the U.S. double-standard is seen in the allocation of resources. Its priorities are established to satisfy the demands of power and greed rather than to address the urgency of human need. Priorities relate to the agenda of manufactured problems while real problems are postponed to that day of wondrous liberation which never comes.

By what twisted logic does a country spend almost as much on armaments at a time in its history when it has no enemies of military significance as it spent at the height of the Cold War? Not only does it defy common sense, it represents a lost opportunity to attack many domestic and global problems that have been crying out for attention.

Look at the contrast. In the Fiscal Year 2002 Discretionary Budget, the U.S. military allocation was $343 billion compared to $45 billion for education, $41 billion for health, and $30 billion for housing.[1] States have been starved for assistance to the point where teachers have been driving school buses and making sandwiches for needy children.

Many other programs have been affected, including road maintenance.[2]

At the same time American aid to poor countries has been far less than might be expected from the world's number one power. In fact, its level of official development assistance in 1997 was absolute bottom of 20 Organization for Economic Cooperation and Development (OECD) countries at 0.08 percent of Gross National Product. This is slightly less than a quarter of Canada's 0.36 percent, but only a tiny fraction of what Sweden, the Netherlands, Norway and Denmark give. These are the only four countries which have reached, or surpassed, the United Nations target of 0.70 percent.[3]

WHAT MIGHT HAVE BEEN

This relative lack of concern for the poor both at home in the United States, and in other less fortunate countries, represents the heart of the moral crisis undermining the legitimacy of U.S. world leadership. In her book entitled *The New Nuclear Danger: George W. Bush's Military-Industrial Complex*, Helen Caldicott sums up the post-cold war decade as "The Tragedy of Lost Opportunities." The tragedy is, alas, bi-partisan.

"Bill Clinton's basic disinterest, distraction, draft handicap, and lack of vision allowed the military – Pentagon, nuclear scientists, and military corporations – to move into this presidential vacuum. They wooed, seduced, and bought Congress and the administrative staff, and the opportunity for nuclear disarmament was tragically lost. Ironically, as we enter the twenty-first century, after eight years of Democratic administration, the world is in a position even more dangerous than it was at the height of Reagan's buildup of nuclear weapons and Star Wars dreams."[4]

At the time of the 2000 presidential election there was no particular reason to believe that a Bush Administration would be either more or less favourable to the Pentagon than its predecessors had been. The world was in for a big surprise, however. For the first time in my memory the Department of Defense has taken charge.

Consequently, instead of cutting defence expenditures significantly, which would have been reasonable in light of the existing realpolitic, they have been increased. This is not in the long-term interest of either the United States or the world. The Pentagon is spending at least $100 billion more each year than can be justified to defend the U.S. and its legitimate interests abroad. Worse, the Future Years Defense Program advocates an addition of $15 to $20 billion a year in a 'topline' increase of $75 billion to $100 billion over the planning period.[5]

Admittedly the recommendation was written at a time when there was a projected budgetary surplus of $700 billion for the same period.[6] Even then, however, there were more pressing needs for the money. Now that the surplus has evaporated, and massive deficits are forecast, the current level of defence expenditure is totally irresponsible. Consequently, it is difficult to comprehend why the Congress would not only approve President Bush's recommended increase for fiscal year 2004, but actually authorize a larger sum than had been requested.

It must have something to do with what U.S. Federal Reserve Chairman Alan Greenspan called Washington's "deafening" silence about the coming challenge to federal finances.[7] The Bush Administration had just shelved a U.S. Treasury report that shows America faces a future of chronic federal budget deficits – totalling at least $44.2 trillion in current dollars.

This massive sum, which is far higher than previous estimates, is the result of an investigation commissioned by former Treasury Secretary Paul O'Neil, and is now known as the Smetters-Gokhale study, the names of its authors. Its chief conclusion is that sharp tax increases or massive spending cuts are unavoidable if the U.S. is to meet the healthcare and retirement benefits promised to future generations. Closing the gap will require the equivalent of an immediate and permanent 70% across-the-board tax rise.[8]

So U.S. citizens have a strong vested interest in an immediate and substantial shift in priorities. They have to do something about that budget deficit or it will just be rolled over into debt – debt on which interest has to be paid. As it is, the citizens of the U.S. will have the dubious privilege of paying for the war on Iraq, for example, not just once, but perhaps two or three times over until the extra debt incurred to finance it has ultimately been repaid.

The poor and dispossessed people of the world also have an abiding interest in U.S. priorities. They look to America, as the unquestioned leader of the world, for help in achieving a better life and, in the case of many millions, of just hanging on to life itself. Imagine what would be possible if the U.S. increased its foreign aid from 0.08 percent of GDP to 0.70 percent in a gesture of generosity comparable to that of Sweden, Denmark, Norway and the Netherlands. The extra $64 billion annually could revolutionize the world.

Within a decade the vast majority of the world's desolate could be transported from a situation of helplessness and hopelessness to a new plateau of hope and realistic expectations for the present and future. They could expect enough food to eat and safe water to drink. They could expect to receive medical attention when sick, and that their children would receive at least a basic education. It would be a revolution on a grander and more glorious scale than ever before. The world would be transformed.

Consider an alternative to the war on Iraq. We were told that it would cost between $72 billion and $80 billion. That does not include the cost of collateral damage and of repairing and rebuilding a decimated economy. But a diversion of even the minimum sum of $72 billion would have been sufficient to finance miracles of gargantuan proportions.

A few years ago the relief organization World Vision estimated that $61 would be enough to save the life of one child. Let's assume that for reasons of inflation and ultra caution that figure is too low and that something of the order of $500 would be more realistic. If you divide $72 billion by $500 you will see that more than 144 million lives could have been saved. Fantastic!

So the question arises, has the military, and Empire building, been given a higher priority than humanity?

CHURCH AND STATE

A characteristic of President George W. Bush that upsets many American liberals is his attempt to associate God with his agenda. It is, alas, the same agenda as that of the military-industrial complex. It is true that the Republic was founded by men who were devoted Christians. But America has changed, and the doctrine of separation of church and state has taken root. Certainly, that is a condition the U.S. wishes to impose on Iraq and other countries.

It is not to say that one is required to leave one's religious beliefs at home when one assumes public office. Rather, it is the sensitivity to acknowledge, as John F. Kennedy did when he was seeking the presidency, that regardless of one's personal beliefs, public office is not the vehicle for imposing one's private practices and mores on others by means of legislation.

In this context it is disconcerting to see George W. Bush invoking God's blessing on the Pentagon's doctrine of preventive wars and a global "constabulary" backed by absolutely incredible military power. I don't pretend to be a Biblical scholar but for the life of me I don't remember reading anything like the following: "Blessed are the warmongers for they shall inherit a world of fear and instability."

Equally distressing is the fact that G.W. Bush was elected with much help from the religious right. One has to ask therefore, if the President's agenda, which is now the U.S. agenda, is their agenda? Is a plan that involves one preventive war and regime change after another, the imposition of American values that include tax cuts for the rich while the poor scramble to keep body and soul together, and the enforcement of American commercial interests around the globe an agenda acceptable to the religious right?

If it is, that would lend credence to the view that the religious right are the Pharisees of the 21st century, a charge some would vehemently deny. "Woe to you, scribes and Pharisees, hypocrites! For you are like whitewashed tombs which indeed appear beautiful outwardly, but inside are full of dead men's bones and all uncleanness."[9]

One of the most disappointing characteristics of the leaders of the religious right has been their analysis of the tragedy of September 11, 2001, including their assessment of the reasons for it. In the view of many, the attacks represented unprovoked evil against a peace and freedom loving country of exemplary morality. No one that I heard or read bothered to point out that Osama bin Laden had learned terrorist tactics from his American tutors. Behaviour that was morally acceptable when it was being used against the Soviets in Afghanistan was re-categorized as infinite evil when directed at the U.S.

A much more insightful analysis was presented by Reverend Doctor Stephen Farris, Professor of Preaching and Worship at Knox College, University of Toronto, in a sermon to Yorkminster Park Baptist Church, in Toronto, on November 11, 2001. The subject was "The Worst Four-Letter Word in the World – HATE!"

Dr. Farris took as his text the 137th Psalm. The children of Israel had been unfaithful to their God, and broken His first commandment, so He allowed evil men to carry them off to Babylon where they sat down and wept when asked to sing the Lord's song. They sought revenge: "Happy shall he be who repays you as you have served us! Happy shall he be who takes and dashes your little ones against the rock."[10]

Dr. Farris emphasized two points. There is precedent for allowing evil to be used to admonish evil. Second, these were religious people who were so full of hate that they would have been happy to see the children of their enemies dashed against the rocks. This kind of hate was not right, Dr. Farris said, but it was real.

I thought of this three days later when the results of a *Christian Science Monitor*/TIPP poll was published. In presenting options for winning the war on terrorism, 60 percent of Americans said they could envision a scenario in which they would support political assassinations. This is in sharp contrast to a 1981 Gallup poll following a decade of widespread criticism of the CIA for promoting that tactic in

Central and South America, when 83 percent said they would
never support political assassinations.[11]

A surprising 32 percent of Americans said they would
support torture of suspects held in the U.S. and abroad.
More than one in four, 27 percent, indicated they would
endorse the use of nuclear weapons – a statistic that fills me
with unspeakable horror. Only 10 percent would support the
use of biological or chemical weapons, a figure which still
appears to be totally inconsistent with the excuse given
subsequently for the war on Iraq.[12]

While such attitudes of hateful revenge are
understandable, they are less so when coming from religious
people of any faith. In preparation for the final chapter of an
earlier book I checked out the principal tenets of each. All
claimed love and charity as paramount. Yet there is scant
evidence of these noble principles finding their way into
public practice. The rhetoric is great – lily white and
laudable. The reality enthrones the gods of power and
mammon.

The religious right believe in an Omnipotent God. So He
could have stopped the horrendous attacks of September 11,
2001. He didn't. Religious leaders owe it to themselves to
ask the question – why not? Was He, one more time,
allowing evil men to deliver a message that desperately needs
to be heard in the corridors of power?

It is my personal opinion, shared by some, but certainly
not by others, that the two greatest concentrations of evil in
the world today are the Pentagon and Wall Street. It could be
less than happenstance that bin Laden selected these two as
symbolic of his hatred for a regime where misrepresentation
and deception are standard operating procedures.

THE PENTAGON

As a former Minister of National Defence who enjoyed
close and cordial relations with the Pentagon throughout my
years in office, it grieves me to conclude that the U.S.
Department of Defense has over-stepped the bounds of
propriety. It has proposed plans for defence systems that
bear no relation to any real military threat to the United

States – and so expensive that not even the world's only superpower can afford them.

More worrisome is its adoption of the strategy of "preventive" wars which was adopted by the Bush Administration in its new National Security Strategy on September 20, 2002. The strategy claims that new threats, including the proliferation of weapons of mass destruction and terrorist networks armed with the agendas of fanatics, are so novel and so dangerous that we should "not hesitate to act alone if necessary, to exercise our right of self-defense by acting pre-emptively."[13]

In the months leading up to the Iraqi war, however, as Senator Edward M. Kennedy pointed out in an address entitled "The Bush Doctrine of Pre-Emption," the administration often used the terms "pre-emptive" and "preventive" interchangeably. "In the realm of international relations, these two terms have long had very different meanings," the Senator stated. He continued:

"Traditionally, 'pre-emptive' action refers to times when states react to an imminent threat of attack. For example, when Egyptian and Syrian forces mobilized on Israel's borders in 1967, the threat was obvious and immediate, and Israel felt justified in pre-emptively attacking those forces. The global community is generally tolerant of such actions, since no nation should have to suffer a certain strike before it has the legitimacy to respond.

"By contrast, 'preventive' military action refers to strikes that target a country before it has developed a capability that could someday become threatening. Preventive attacks have generally been condemned. For example, the 1941 sneak attack on Pearl Harbor was regarded as a preventive strike by Japan, because the Japanese were seeking to block a planned military buildup by the United States in the Pacific.

"The coldly premeditated nature of preventive attacks and preventive wars makes them anathema to well-established international principles against aggression. Pearl Harbor has been rightfully recorded in history as an act of dishonorable treachery.

"Historically, the United States has condemned the idea of preventive war, because it violates basic international rules against aggression. But at times in our history, preventive war has been seriously advocated as a policy option."[14] The Senator went on to explain that in each case the temptation was resisted and wiser heads prevailed.

"In today's context, it is impossible to justify any such double standard under international law. Might does not make right. America cannot write its own rules for the modern world ... The Administration's doctrine is a call for 21st century American imperialism that no other nation can or should accept. It is the antithesis of all that America has worked so hard to achieve in international relations since the end of World War II."[15] (Senator Kennedy's speech is so important and so relevant to the peace and security of the world that I have attached it as Appendix A.)

The Pentagon has, knowingly or otherwise, usurped the power of the civil authorities by rejecting the lessons from history and preparing a blueprint for global domination through the application of military force. That is what the document "Rebuilding America's Defenses: Strategy, Forces and Resources for a New Century" really is. It is a plan for empire-building under false pretences. Under the guise of defending America and its interests, the Pentagon has launched a plan of offence and intervention designed to enforce American values and, worse, its commercial interests on a reluctant world.

I will argue in the next section that the kind of empire under construction is basically a global piracy which allows U.S. commercial and financial interests to pillage and plunder the assets of poorer countries everywhere. The designation of such an empire as an "Evil Empire" is not unjust. It is a literal assessment of the reality.

Of the evil means of enforcement being developed by the Pentagon, weapons of mass destruction are the most offensive. One can understand the U.S. fixation on these weapons because no country has larger stockpiles of chemical, biological and nuclear devices than it does. No country is spending as much to increase the deadliness and havoc-creating capacity of each. Most alarming, no country except the United States has even hinted that they would consider "first use" of atomic devices.

I had long been convinced that no civilized country would ever again consider the use of atomic weapons except in response to an attack. How can there be people so blind to the potential consequences, and so totally immune to any feeling for the welfare of humankind, that they could even think of such a monstrous act.

I was shocked to learn that the U.S. Department of Energy's nuclear laboratories at Los Alamos and Sandia in New Mexico, and Lawrence Livermore in California, had embarked on a second "Manhattan Project" costing 5 to 6 billion dollars a year for the next ten to fifteen years, to design, test and develop new nuclear weapons under the guise of ensuring the safety and reliability of the existing U.S. stockpile.[16] Why would the U.S. spend untold billions of dollars developing weapons which sane men decided decades ago could not and would not be used?

The answer came when I read, with horror, that the Bush Administration is reassessing America's nuclear arsenal with an eye toward smaller bombs to combat 21st century perils.[17] Talk about a double standard! Here is the U.S. prepared to go to war to limit nuclear proliferation while developing new weapons for its own use.

"They are seeking to make these weapons more usable and are thinking about these as just another kind of weapon in our arsenal,"[18] said Daryl Kimball, executive director of the Arms Control Association.

"And that kind of thinking is dangerous. It promotes proliferation. And it's unnecessary given our overwhelming conventional superiority. This is the classic case of capability overkill. The Pentagon says it is aiming to modernize a Cold War arsenal to meet 21st century threats. Defense Secretary Donald Rumsfeld has argued that potential adversaries, knowing U.S. precision weapons can hit almost any target at any time, are seeking to make military assets invulnerable by burying them deep underground, including facilities to make and store chemical and biological arms.

"Pentagon leaders say nuclear weapons may provide an effective way to destroy such bunkers and wipe out enemy stocks of chemical weapons and disease-spreading biological agents. During the Cold War, the vast Soviet nuclear arsenal was deemed the prime threat to America. The Pentagon, in a statement to Reuters explaining U.S. nuclear policy, said the new threat is posed by what it calls rogue states and terrorist groups armed with weapons of mass destruction."[19]

They can't be serious, I thought, at first glance. But it is the U.S. Department of Defense speaking, and they are serious.

Of all the Pentagon's abhorrent plans the one to weaponize space has to be the most repugnant. Star Wars has emerged from the twilight zone and once again enjoys top billing on the Pentagon marquee. The transformation is another classic case of subterfuge, deception and outright lies.

Initially the product was billed as a National Missile Defense, a narrow, well-defined nuclear shield designed to protect the continental United States from a stray missile or two fired in its direction from what it designated as 'rogue states" – North Korea being the least improbable.

From the outset I said and wrote that this was not the real intent. It was just a decoy to get all of the political ducks lined up and quacking in chorus. Such a modest proposal, with limited objectives, and at modest cost – in defence terms – couldn't be resisted.

It was only after people began reading "Rebuilding America's Defenses," and the U.S. began negotiating with other countries, especially Russia, that the full scope of the project began to emerge. The White House was finally forced to acknowledge at least part of the truth with its press release of December 17, 2002 where the President said:

"Because the threats of the 21st century also endanger our friends and allies around the world, it is essential that we work together to defend against them. The Defense Department will develop and deploy missile defenses capable of protecting not only the United States and our deployed forces, but also our friends and allies."[20]

The Pentagon, at least, has been more open about its objectives. "Building an effective, robust, layered, global system of missile defenses is a prerequisite for maintaining American preeminence," their planning document says.[21] "Unrestricted use of space has become a major strategic interest of the United States," the document adds.[22] This is not a plan to protect the continental United States, it is a program to eliminate the ability of all countries, everywhere, to deter U.S. blackmail.

So the Pentagon is determined to occupy the military "high ground," which in my opinion equates with the moral low ground, by establishing a new service called "Space Command." Its mission is not to guarantee the peaceful uses of space in the interests of all mankind, it will be "the ability to assure access to space, freedom of operations within the space medium, and an ability to deny others the use of space."[23] One set of rules for the U.S., and another for all other countries.

These are big plans. At an Air Force Briefing on "Space: The Warfighter's Perspective," Maj.Gen. Franklin J. Blaisdell, the director of Space Operations and Integration for the Air Force, said: "Ladies and gentlemen, space truly is a worldwide mission. We've got 33,600 folks spread in 21 different locations here in the United States and 15 [other] places around the world. So you're dealing with a real synergistic effort here. It's not just the continental United States."[24] The General gave his assessment of things present and things to come: "Whether it's Iraq or any enemy of the United States and its allies, I would tell you that we are so dominant in space that I pity a country that would come up against us."[25] (U.S. Air Force emphasis.)

What the Pentagon plans to do, if Congress continues to provide the funding, is to build a first strike capability that would allow it to incinerate any country on the planet without fear that the U.S. would automatically suffer a similar fate as was the case during the Cold War.

I have always considered this prospect as inherently evil. No country has the moral integrity that would be prerequisite for the custodian of such power. As Dr. Helen Caldicott, author of *The New Nuclear Danger,* points out: "A huge conventional and nuclear arsenal allows America to do what it will around the world with impunity – the iron hand in the velvet glove of U.S. corporate globalization."[26]

As I will argue in the next chapter, corporate globalization is not really a velvet glove. It is Wall Street's evil brew concocted by the same sorcerers responsible for the Pentagon's plans.

CHAPTER 6

WALL STREET AND THE AXIS OF EVIL

"The new world without borders will be like a zoo without cages. Only the most powerful of the species will survive."

Paul Hellyer

If the brainwashing techniques used to convince millions of people that the war on Iraq was all about weapons of mass destruction worked well as planned, then it is fair to say that the success of those same techniques in convincing the majority that globalization is both inevitable and good, has been even better. It is proof positive of the old adage that if you tell a lie big enough and often enough people will believe it.

In fact, globalization, as presently being rammed down the throats of helpless millions of people, is neither inevitable nor good. It is only inevitable if we let it happen, and it is only good for a very small minority – perhaps 2 to 5 percent of the world's population.

In general, the benefits flow to those who are already rich and powerful, while the majority are worse off, some of them disastrously so. Consequently, when you read a column or an editorial that includes a phrase like "the unquestionable benefits of globalization," you can be certain that you are reading something written by someone who, in all probability, has not given the subject as much as half an hour of what I would call "deep thought."

It is important to   point out at the outset that "globalization" is not just one great big ball of wax. An analogy I find useful is to compare it to cholesterol. There is good cholesterol and bad cholesterol. The good cholesterol is life-enhancing, whereas the bad cholesterol can kill you.

Similarly there is good globalization and bad globalization. The good globalization is technologically driven. The internet, for example, apart from its addictive qualities and the temptation to wander off in search of pornography or gambling, is a marvelous benefit of technology. It opens up a whole new world of knowledge and information on a scale hitherto undreamed of. And its benefits are widely dispersed; this book would have taken two or three times as long to complete without the benefit of the internet. Satellite phones are another useful marvel.

These widely enjoyed benefits are in sharp contrast to the bad globalization which is agenda driven. It is the coldly calculated business plan of the richest most powerful people in the world to re-engineer the global economy and governance in a way that will increase their overly-generous slice of the economic pie even further.

In theory, the New World Order, as President George W. Bush called it, is a world without economic borders. It is a kind of *laissez-faire* economic Darwinism, where capital is king of the jungle. It has been labelled neo-classical economics, a revised but unrepentant version of the ideas of Milton Friedman and his colleagues at the University of Chicago, and sometimes as The Washington Consensus, the rules by which the world must be run. Whatever the tag, the transformation now underway is so far-reaching as to be almost beyond belief.

If allowed to run its course, no municipality will be able to favour a local contractor; no country will be able to protect its industries even long enough for them to mature to the point where they could compete in a global market. Neither could any nation state set higher environmental standards than the market would tolerate, nor legislate to protect its labour from exploitation for fear of losing jobs to another country where Dickensian standards remain in effect.

No country would be able to prevent the sale of an industry to a big foreign player wishing to: (a) include it in its empire, or (b) shut it down to eliminate the competition, or

(c) move it to another country where lower wages and environmental standards would permit higher profits. Foreigners will be able to buy your natural resources and export them without any value added.

Under rules currently being negotiated at the World Trade Organization, outsiders will demand that government subsidies now available for public health, public education, public transport, public sewers and water systems be made equally available to them to provide private health care, private education, private water systems and so on. The theory is to commodify everything and eliminate, to the maximum extent possible, any public involvement.

Under its benevolent wrapping, globalization is a plan to strip elected representatives at all levels of government of their power to legislate on behalf of ordinary people, and to transfer that power to unelected, unaccountable international bureaucrats implementing rules laid down by the globalizers. It is a plan to end popular democracy as we have known it, and substitute a plutocracy of the wealthy elite.

It doesn't require much imagination to understand what the New World Order will be like. For most people it will be a life of total powerlessness. There will be little point in looking to your alderman, member of the legislature or member of parliament for help because in many cases they will say, as has already happened, we are powerless because we are bound by international treaties that take precedence. In fact there will be little point in running for public office and putting up with the frustration of having your hands tied in advance.

In the case of small and medium powers, like Canada, there will be the added frustration of seeing the level of excellence already achieved slowly ebbing away, and with it their significance as a nation state. As companies are bought by foreigners, and head offices move, the good jobs disappear. The tax base is also eroded because foreign-owned companies pay less tax than domestically-owned companies.

At the same time, one country after another is losing its right to use its own central bank to help finance essential services when the tax revenue from other sources is being eroded.   It is not by accident that countries are being encouraged to adopt either the U.S. dollar or the Euro as a replacement for their own currency.   It is all part of the scheme to rob people of their assets so the rich can second them – a scam to which I shall return later.

BRAINWASHING

You may well wonder how such a grand larceny, on a global scale, could be sold to an unsuspecting public. So too, apparently, did its sponsors.

Gregory Palast, author of *The Best Democracy Money Can Buy*, and whistle-blower extraordinaire, has unearthed some fascinating information about secret meetings between European and American captains of industry and finance. He even managed to get minutes of some of their meetings. In an interview with *Acres USA*, Palast had this to say:

"One of the most amazing things in one of these meetings is when they talk about how to sell globalization to the public. They can't figure out how to sell this thing to the public because they can't figure out what the benefits of globalization really are to the average person. They actually sat there and said: 'Why don't we pay some professors a bunch of money, and get them to come up with a study that globalization is good for people?'

"Then the officer for Reuters, the big news service that's in every big paper on the planet, said: 'You come up with the material and we'll help you out, we'll place the stories in our papers.' It really freaked me out to find this propaganda system to sell people on the means of their own economic destruction."[1]

I don't know why Palast was so surprised. The neo-cons, who are mostly a bunch of very rich old cons, have been peddling their propaganda for decades. And they have provided a real "bunch of money" to hire dozens of accommodating professors to write myriad papers proving beyond reasonable doubt that black is white.

As far back as 1943, a group of anti-New Deal businessmen established the American Enterprise Institute. It provided intellectual public relations in the 1950s and 1960s working directly with members of Congress, the federal bureaucracy and the media.[2]

The Heritage Foundation is another one of the best-known U.S. think tanks because of its close association with Ronald Reagan, and its powerful influence on his policies. Its success inspired the creation of 37 mini-Heritages across the U.S. providing synergy, an illusion of diversity and the impression that the experts quoted actually represented a broad spectrum of views. Other, smaller, U.S. think tanks include the venerable Hoover Institution on War, Revolution and Peace; the Cato Institute and the Manhattan Institute for Policy Research.[3]

The United Kingdom has its own network including the Centre for Policy Studies; the anti-Statist Institute of Economic Affairs; and the Adam Smith Institute. Even Canada is not immune from the propaganda factories. We have the very influential Fraser Institute in British Columbia; the C.D. Howe Institute in Toronto; and a number of new regional institutes based on the same model.

These institutions have much in common. They are financed by foundations and large corporations which are anti-populist in philosophy. In general they believe that the least government is the best government; that nation states have outlived their usefulness; that markets are infallible regulators of economic activity; and that the rich have no obligation to share their wealth with the poor on whom they depend for labour and as customers for their goods and services.

This, then, is the philosophy of the captains of industry and finance that Gregory Palast said had been meeting secretly to promote their globalization agenda. These same people, who are re-engineering the world for their own benefit, have no compunction about using both governments and international institutions as water boys to carry their bats for them. They use them to promote international treaties that diminish the power of nation states to act on behalf of their citizens; to jaw-bone poor countries into selling their assets at firesale prices; and to help enforce contracts even when those contracts were not negotiated in good faith and were much more favourable to one side than the other. As Joseph E. Stiglitz, former chief economist of the World Bank, says: "There is, in fact, a long history of 'unfair' contracts, which western governments have used their muscle to enforce."[4]

THE AXIS OF EVIL – THE IMF, WORLD BANK, AND WTO

If President George W. Bush wants to find the real axis of evil he has only to look at three international organizations which, in their present incarnations, are the progeny of previous U.S. administrations, and are now the adopted children of his own. I refer to the International Monetary Fund, the Bank for Reconstruction and Development (World Bank), and the World Trade Organization.

In a previous book I refer to the first two, the IMF and the World Bank, as "The Enforcers" of globalization. They are the bullies that carry the big sticks and beat the bejeebers out of any country that won't adopt the Washington Consensus and open its borders to rape and pillage by international banks and multinational corporations. The Enforcers work hand and glove with the U.S. Department of the Treasury (DOT) and Wall Street, for which the DOT acts as agent.

The World Trade Organization is a new addition to the evil axis. It has earned this distinction for actions past, present and planned. It has been enforcing global rules, written by or for Wall Street moguls, for the benefit of the industrial heavyweights at the expense of the lightweights and featherweights. It has invariably ruled in favour of commerce at the expense of the environment and, finally, the rules currently being negotiated under the General Agreement on Trade in Services (GATS) will remove from legislators in nation states most of their residual power to act on behalf of their electors. So the WTO has to be admitted as a member of the club but, for now, we should concentrate on the frightening record of the other two.

Both were born in 1944 at the Bretton Woods Conference and both had laudable mandates. The IMF lost its *raison d'être* however, when most of the world switched from fixed to floating exchange rates, and it was no longer necessary to provide temporary cash to prevent a devaluation. The World Bank, meanwhile, borrowed money on world financial markets and lent it to Third World countries to build roads, bridges and dams – especially dams – until those countries were up to their eyeballs in debt.

They were just able to take an occasional breath in order to survive when along came the monetarist economics of Milton Friedman and his colleagues, with its ridiculously high interest rates, and they were swamped. Servicing enormous debt at 5 or 6 percent interest was extremely difficult. To pay 18%, after U.S. Federal Reserve Board Chairman Paul Volcker raised rates to that dizzying height in 1980, was impossible! Absolutely impossible!

It was Volcker's subsequent determination to rescue the investment of his New York banker friends, that had been put in jeopardy by his interest rate policy, which led to the scam which led to the grand larceny of the 1980s, 1990s and beyond. Chairman Volcker realized that several South American countries were technically bankrupt. He also realized that all of the major New York banks were technically insolvent as a consequence. So he forced the banks to lend those countries more money, so they could pay the interest on their existing debt until he could persuade the IMF to ride to the rescue with taxpayers' money. That way the loans would appear to be performing when, in fact, they were non-performing. Had the public been exposed to the truth, there might have been a financial panic.

The IMF did in fact ride to the rescue of the poor countries but not in order to save those countries. It was to rescue the foreign investors. At last it had found a new *raison d'être*. It would be the life-raft for international capital to see it safely home after being invested irresponsibly in Third World countries.

The IMF performed this role so well that it was recruited by Wall Street and the U.S. Treasury Department to become the sword-carrier for the imposition of the Washington Consensus on financially destitute countries everywhere. Its "success" was so great that it eventually ran out of money. Consequently its sponsors had to persuade the World Bank, too, to abandon its traditional role and learn the skills of a sword-bearer on behalf of market fundamentalism.

The Washington Consensus became synonymous with market fundamentalism, and the principal American intellectual export since anti-communism lost its currency. Widely known as the Washington Consensus, and sometimes simply as "free trade," this gospel has become the basis for an American "Crusade" to "liberate" people everywhere, and save them from their poverty and archaic economic notions – the latter obviously considered as cause and effect in the minds of the "liberators." William Finnegan, in an article entitled "The Economics of Power," published in *Harper's* magazine, describes the strategic battle plan.

"It [The Washington Consensus] is promulgated directly through U.S. foreign policy and indirectly through multilateral institutions such as the World Bank, the International Monetary Fund, and the World Trade Organization. Its core tenets are deregulation, privatization, 'openness' (to foreign investment, and to exports [from foreign countries]), unrestricted movement of capital, and lower taxes. Presented with special force to developing countries as a formula, a theory, of how the world should be run, under American supervision. Attacking America is, therefore, attacking the theory, and attacking the theory is attacking America."[5]

The theory has now been in effect in varying degrees for 30 years since the central banks of the western world adopted the monetarist, "markets in, governments out" ideas of Milton Friedman and his colleagues in 1974; and in dead earnest for more than 20 years since Friedman's disciple Paul Volcker decided to put monetarist theories to the test. The time has come to apply the old adage, "The test of the pudding is in the eating." The theory has been given ample opportunity to demonstrate its worth. A few examples, of what could be an entire book on the subject, are illustrative.

In exchange for financial assistance from the World Bank and the IMF the Government of Tanzania was required to agree to 157 conditions. Trade barriers were cut, government subsidies were restricted and state industries were sold off. In just 15 years, according to Nancy Alexander of the Washington-based Globalization Challenge Institute, Tanzania's GDP dropped from $309 to $210 per capita, the literacy rate is falling and the rate of abject poverty has jumped to 51 percent of the population.[6]

Bolivia is a country of great natural wealth but where nearly all the benefit goes to foreigners. When it emerged from many years of military rule in the early 1980s the country was in deep trouble due to looting by the generals. Its foreign debt was overwhelming and its annual rate of inflation was 24,000 percent. It was ripe for the radical treatment recommended by the young American economist Jeffrey Sacks, who later became known for designing "shock therapy" plans for countries emerging from communism – which some have credited with the near-destruction of the Russian economy.

For Bolivia the therapy included a drastic devaluation of the currency, abolition of minimum wages, and drastic cutbacks in government expenditures. As a result the country was plunged into a deep recession. Wages fell and unemployment skyrocketed. But prices were stabilized and the Bolivian Government's good relations with its foreign creditors, and especially with "The Enforcers" were restored.

World Bank development loans helped keep the country afloat, but it and the IMF took control of large areas of public policy. Like many poor countries, Bolivia was subjected to the rigors of market fundamentalism, a term William Finnegan describes as: "a set of standardized, far-reaching austerity and 'openness' measures that typically include the removal of restrictions on foreign investment, the abolition of public subsidies and labor rights, reduced state spending, deregulation, lower tariffs, tighter credit, the encouragement of export-oriented industries, lower marginal tax rates, currency devaluation, and the sale of major public enterprises. In Bolivia's case, the latter included the national railways, the national airlines, the telephone system, the country's vast tin mines, and a long list of municipal utilities."[7]

Now, the people of Bolivia work at low wages for the benefit of foreign capitalists who rely on the World Bank and the IMF to provide *de facto* government that best suits their interests rather than the real interests of the Bolivian people.

Argentina has been a test case for economic fundamentalism, and the New World Order. It did everything right throughout the 1990s – privatization, deregulation, trade liberalization, tax reform – and became Exhibit A for the true believers in *laissez-faire* economics, until shortly before its collapse in 2001. Since then it has become Exhibit A for those who say that monetarism or neo-liberalism – whatever you want to call it – is junk economics.

In early 2002 Gregory Palast got inside documents from Argentina outlining the secret plan for that country which had been signed by Jim Wolfensohn, the President of the World Bank. As part of its integration into the New World Order, Argentina was required by the IMF and the World Bank to sell off all its major public assets. Palast talks about some of the implications in an interview with Alex Jones.

"It's not just anyone who gets a piece of the action. The water system of Buenos Aires was sold off for a song to a company called Enron. A pipeline, that runs between Argentina and Chile, was sold to Enron."[8]

Palast continued: "I actually spoke to a senator from Argentina two weeks ago. [February 2002] I got him on camera. He said that after he got a call from George W. Bush in 1988 saying give the gas pipeline in Argentina to Enron, that's our current president. He said that what he found was really creepy, was that Enron was going to pay one-fifth of the world's price for the gas and he said how can you make such an offer? And he was told, not by George W. but by a partner in the deal, well if we only pay one-fifth that leaves quite a little bit for you to go in your Swiss bank account. And that's how it's done... They hand it over, generally, to the cronies like Citibank [which] was very big and grabbed half the Argentine banks. You've got British Petroleum grabbing pipelines in Equador."[9]

Palast pointed out, by way of background, that the United States is a major financial contributor to both the IMF and the World Bank.

"So the question becomes, what are we getting for the money we put in there? And it looks like we are getting mayhem in several nations. Indonesia is in flames. He was telling me, [Joseph Stiglitz, former chief economist of the World Bank], that he started questioning what was happening. You know, everywhere we go, every country we end up meddling in, we destroy their economy and they end up in flames.

"And he [Stiglitz] was saying that he questioned this, and he got fired for it. He was saying that they even kind of plan in the riots. They know that when they squeeze a country and destroy its economy, you are going to get riots in the streets. And they say, well that's the IMF riot. In other words, because you have a riot you lose. All the capital runs away from your country and that gives the opportunity for the IMF to then add more conditions."[10]

While Palast drives home his points with flamboyant language, economist Stiglitz confirms the substance in his more scholarly style. In *Globalization and its Discontents* he writes: "(As of January 2002, Argentina is going through a crisis. Once again, the IMF bailout policies failed to work; the contradictory fiscal policies that it insisted upon pushed the economy into an ever deeper recession.) The IMF never asked why its models systematically underestimated the depth of recessions – or why its policies are systematically excessively contradictory."[11]

If globalization and "free trade" are creating poverty, misery, corruption and mayhem on an ever-widening scale, they are also producing economic results that are far less satisfactory than those achieved before the new [old] economic fundamentalism was adopted as holy writ.

The compound annual growth rate of U.S. Gross National Product in the bad old days from 1948 to 1973, before the monetarist counter-revolution conquered the hearts and minds of policy makers, was 3.70 percent. From 1974 to 2001 the GDP grew by an average of 2.9 percent – a reduction of 22 percent.[12] For Canada, the growth rate from 1949 to 1973 averaged 4.9 percent compared to 3.03 percent during the 1974-2001 Friedman era – a reduction of 38 percent.[13]

Latin America and Africa have fared much worse. In those dark ages of increasing national government control and ownership (1960-1980), per capita income grew by 73 percent in Latin America and by 34 percent in Africa. By comparison, since 1980, Latin American growth has come to a virtual halt, growing by less than 6 percent over 20 years – and African incomes have declined by 23 percent.[14]

Obviously market fundamentalism, like other fundamentalisms, is impervious to argument or inconvenient facts. So how do they sell it? Invariably professors attempting to make a case will go back to 1950 for their data. It is convenient, but dishonest, to use the successes of the Keynesian interventionist years to justify the failures of a model which, as Joseph Stiglitz says, doesn't make sense outside the classroom. Listen to William Finnegan's concerns.

"But vulgarity and obtuseness should not be mistaken for sincerity. Not only is the case for President Bush's 'opinion' that 'free trade is good for both wealthy and impoverished nations' empirically feeble; there is plenty of evidence that rich countries, starting with the United States, have no intention of playing by the trade rules and strictures they foist on poorer, weaker countries as 'a single sustainable model.' We practice free trade selectively, which is to say not at all, and, when it suits our commercial purposes, we actively prevent poor countries from exploiting their few advantages on world markets."[15]

The extent of the economic terrorism is all pervasive. The IMF and World Bank not only put poor countries in economic straight-jackets, they lock them tight by refusing to let those countries use their own central banks to create money to help finance the cost of health care and education. Ironically, this is the issue on which the U.S. War for Independence was fought.

Although we were taught that the argument was about tea, that was far from the whole story. True, tea was a factor because it was supplied by one of the U.K. monopolies which exploited the colonists in a manner not too different from the way U.S. multinationals are exploiting their "colonists." But in his memoirs, Benjamin Franklin tells us that the real issue was London's decision that the colonies could no longer print their own money.

They had been doing this successfully for some years, especially in Pennsylvania where "ship-building prospered and both exports and imports increased markedly."[16] Even Adam Smith, who was not a fan of government-created money, admitted that Pennsylvania's paper currency "is said never to have sunk below the value of the gold and silver which was current in the colony before the first issue of paper money."[17]

Unfortunately the London bankers found out about it and insisted that Westminster pass a law forbidding the practice. Instead of creating their own money, the colonists were forced to borrow from London banks and repay principal and interest in gold that they didn't have. A depression resulted and when the colonists decided on another currency issue war became inevitable.

Substitute Wall Street for London, and the underdeveloped world for the American colonies, and you have a picture of the scene in the world today. Now, as in the time of the American War for Independence, economic terrorism is backed by military force. But today the U.S. has such overwhelming military power that no country, either poor or relatively well to do, can challenge it. And if Wall Street's industrial-military complex has its way, no one will ever be able to.

As long as financial power is concentrated on Wall Street, the impoverished people of the world will have to choose between a form of perpetual slavery, or the loss of most or all of their natural assets – or, in far too many cases, both. It is all embodied in the Project for a New American Century which is the cocaine of the economic fundamentalist marauders, but arsenic for the rest of the world.

Little wonder that even the Hungarian-born American financier George Soros is concerned. Speaking of his student days and recalling a book entitled *Open Society and its Enemies*, by Karl Popper, Soros says: "At that time, open society was threatened by various totalitarian ideologies – fascism, Nazism and communism – which used the power of the state to impose their final solutions. Open society is now also threatened from the opposite direction, from what I call market fundamentalism. I used to call it *laissez-faire* but I prefer market fundamentalism because *laissez-faire* is a French expression and most market fundamentalists don't speak French."[18]

Call it what you like, "the single sustainable model for national success" – the Washington Consensus – is being imposed on the world through the diplomatic and military power of the United States. It is in all respects a totalitarian ideology which rejects all others. It is anathema to open societies, just as fascism and communism have been.

For that reason, Canadians have to ask themselves whether or not they want to be part of the New American Empire. And if not, are they willing to take back enough sovereignty to be in a position to adopt and promote a better, fairer way – a world of diversity where everyone has the right to experiment with new solutions and succeed or fail without fear of intolerable interference from abroad.

It is impossible to build a fair and just world of opportunity without giving back to nation states more power over their own affairs, including the right to create their own money!

I repeat for emphasis:

It is impossible to build a fair and just world of opportunity without giving back to nation states more power over their own affairs, including the right to create their own money!

Before one can understand the full significance of that statement, however, it is necessary to understand where money comes from – which, regrettably, the majority do not.

CHAPTER 7

WHERE DOES MONEY COME FROM?

"The process by which banks create money is so simple the mind is repelled. Where something so important is involved, a deeper mystery seems only decent."[1]

J.K. Galbraith

It must be the simplicity, as Galbraith suggests, that repels the mind. I have, or at least used to have, quite a few intelligent friends, most of them well-educated university graduates. But as soon as I would mention the word money, and where it comes from, they would freak out. Eyes would roll and body language would signal acute boredom.

The mystery deepens when I realize that they know little if anything about the subject. This includes most community leaders many of whom I interviewed when I was writing my first book on the subject in 1993 – newspaper publishers, editors-in-chief and even well-known financial writers. They presume to tell the government how the country should be run without, themselves, possessing a working knowledge of the most potent weapon in the federal government's economic arsenal – money.

Money is the gasoline for the economic engine. If there is too much of it, the engine will flood – we call it inflation. If there is too little, the engine will sputter, lose power and operate far below its potential. Whether this results in a great depression, a great recession like the one in 1981-82, a milder recession or simply stagnation, as we see in various economies in the early years of the 21st century, depends on the magnitude of the shortfall.

The sad part of this story, as anyone familiar with economic history will know, is that we nearly always suffer either feast or famine. There is either too much money chasing too few goods and services, or too many goods being produced and not enough money to buy them. And this has been the case for at least 200 years, ever since the Industrial Revolution began. The people who are paid to do the thinking have never been able to get it right – at least for very long.

This includes some of the best known names in economics including John Maynard Keynes and Milton Friedman. Of the two, Keynes' contribution was at least positive – a step forward. He recognized and confirmed what mavericks like me had been saying for generations. From time to time there was a shortage of purchasing power – what the economists call "aggregate demand." In layman's language there was not enough money available to buy all the goods on store shelves.

Classical economists, who are best known for taking in each other's washing, insisted that this was impossible. They clung stubbornly to what was known as Say's Law, the brainchild of economist Jean Baptiste Say. Say proclaimed that all production created an equal and opposite demand. Consequently, there could be no such thing as a shortage of purchasing power. His colleagues, without taking time out to think about it, agreed.

If Keynes analyzed the problem correctly, and gave legitimacy to views that had long been dismissed as heresy, or worse, his solution was an expedient which produced immediate positive results but which didn't address the fundamental question which was at the root of the problem.

Keynes suggested that in times of recession governments should increase their spending with money that they would get through borrowing, rather than by means of taxation. The extra spending would provide the purchasing power necessary to provide jobs for the unemployed and get the old economic engine back up to full power. Once the economy was operating on all cylinders, taxes should be raised to pay off the debt incurred in the process.

A problem arose when experience showed that it wasn't possible to raise taxes enough to retire the debt without taking so much money out of peoples' wallets that they didn't have enough left to pay for all of the increased production. So unemployment would start to rise and the whole cycle would start all over again. Keynes was correct about the shortage of purchasing power, but he didn't tackle the thornier issue of why that was so.

If Keynes gave us half a loaf of hope, Milton Friedman has the dubious distinction of coming along and taking it all away from us. Seldom, if ever, has so much damage been done to as many people around the world as he and his colleagues at the University of Chicago have done. They have moved us back to the pre-Keynesian, pre-Great Depression system of *laissez-faire* Darwinian economics. The result has been high unemployment, slower economic growth worldwide and an ever-increasing mountain of debt which is politically, economically, and mathematically impossible to pay off.

Friedman and the Chicago School (the second one, the first one of the 1930s made a lot of good sense) made a couple of cardinal errors. The first was the attempt to make a science of a discipline that is more properly called political economy. This required them to produce complex mathematical models that are good fun for mathematicians, but which are the kiss of death in economics because they are classroom extractions that don't relate to the real world.

The other fundamental error was Friedman's misdiagnosis of the inflation of the late '60s and early '70s. He claimed that it was classic inflation, defined as too much money chasing too few goods. He couldn't have been more wrong. The supermarkets were crammed with goods, and small stores were going bankrupt every day for lack of customers for their wares. The facts refuted Friedman's thesis, but that didn't matter to the Chicago School or to the Nobel Committee which adopted its ideas as the new truth in economics.

Friedman sold his theory to thousands of students on the basis of his research which had showed that for a hundred

years in a hundred countries prices had risen in direct
proportion to the amount of money created. While it may be
true that figures don't lie, they don't always reveal the whole
truth either. In this case Friedman's observations are about
as helpful as the discovery that for a hundred years in a
hundred countries summer followed winter.

That, too, is true but it doesn't tell you whether the
summers were too hot and dry, too cool and wet, or just
about the right balance for abundant crops. The devil is in
the details and Friedman completely overlooked a new
phenomenon that had profoundly influenced prices in the '60s
and '70s. For the first time in recorded economic history
nominal wages in Western countries had risen by a multiple
of productivity for 25 consecutive years.

It had been this disconnect between wages and
productivity which had been primarily responsible for the
inflation of those years. True, there were a couple of blips
caused by increases in oil prices when the Organization of
Petroleum Exporting Countries (OPEC) got its act together.
But this was never responsible for more than a small fraction
of the inflation. Nor was the Vietnam War the culprit, as
most orthodox economists insisted.

The data from 15 Organization for Economic Cooperation and Development (OECD) countries shows clearly
that the principal cause of inflation in the '50s, '60s and '70s
was nominal wages rising faster than productivity. The
average of averages for fifteen countries showed that prices
rose by the difference between the average increase in
nominal wages, and the average increase in real output per
member of the labour force, within one-quarter of one
percent, which is about as close as you can get in economics.

The arithmetic is simple. If each of us, on average,
produces less than 2% more goods and services than we did
the year before, as was the case in the United States and
Canada from 1964 to 1991, how large a real wage increase
can we have? The answer is, less than 2 percent, on average.
Anything more than that creates inflation – of the cost-push
variety.

The problem with mis-diagnosis, in economics as in medicine, is that prescribing the wrong medication can produce excruciatingly painful results. So when Friedman's disciple Paul Volcker, Chairman of the Federal Reserve Board in the United States, Gerald Bouey, Governor of the Bank of Canada, and other central bankers cut off the money supply in 1981-82, to cause the worst recession since the Great Depression of the 1930s, the results were disastrous.

Economies were strangled, growth rates plummeted, government revenues fell dramatically and deficits soared; these were rolled over into debt which compounded at the artificially high interest rates, and headed to heights that have put the world in hock to the money lenders. Sadly, as we were just beginning to recover from that smashing blow, the central bankers did it to us again in 1990-91, and the world economy is still reeling from the cumulative effects.

The social consequences of the two recessions were equally profound. Millions of people lost their jobs, countless thousands lost their houses because they couldn't afford the high interest rates on the mortgages, and thousands of young entrepreneurs lost their fledgling and in some cases even mature businesses when fidgety banks called their loans. Perhaps the saddest commentary of all, is that more than a decade later central bankers, steeped in the Friedman dogma, still don't understand either the real nature of the problem or the appropriate policy mix necessary to cope.

Once the mystery of modern inflation is mastered, we can move on to the more fundamental question of what money really is. The biggest failure of all major economic schools is their steadfast refusal to face the 6 trillion dollar question head on. They will not admit the obvious fact than an economic system where nearly all of the new money is created as debt is neither a good system nor a sustainable one.

THE NATURE OF MONEY

When most "money" was gold, silver, copper or iron coins the system was much easier to understand. Usually the minting of money was a monopoly of the monarch and counterfeiters were severely dealt with. As economies became larger and more complex, however, the supply of coins became inadequate and the efficiency of using them for large transactions became increasingly hopeless.

So the system evolved in the direction of one where paper money became dominant and, more recently, electronic money has been displacing paper. Coins have been relegated to the "small change" category. While it is fair to say that the system has evolved to meet changing needs, it is equally fair to say that it has just grown like Topsy, without any visible tutor or headmaster.

The history of money is really fascinating, and I have written more extensively on the subject in other books. For present purposes, however, it may be sufficient just to turn the clock back about 300 years to the time when the Bank of England was chartered as a solution to a serious dilemma.

King William's War, 1688-1697, proved to be much more costly than anticipated. As a result, much of England's gold and silver had to be shipped to the continent in payment of debt. This reduced the money supply in England, and the economy suffered accordingly. Something had to be done to keep the wheels of commerce turning. A bright entrepreneur came up with the idea of establishing a bank to help fill the void. So the Bank of England was chartered.

The scheme involved an initial subscription of £1,200,000 in gold and silver which would be lent to the government at 8 percent. That appeared to be fair enough, although the interest rate was really quite high for a government-guaranteed investment. That was only the beginning, however, because in addition to a £4,000 management fee, the Bank of England was granted an advantage only available to banks and bankers. It was granted authority to issue "banknotes" in an amount equal to its capital and lend the notes into circulation at high interest rates. This was not the first case of paper money issued by private banks in the modern era, but it was the first of great and lasting significance in the English-speaking world.[2]

THE BANKING SCAM

Please note that the Bank of England was allowed to print the £1,200,000 in banknotes that they lent into circulation. The only immediate cost involved was the cost of the paper. Thus began what economists subsequently labelled "the fractional reserve" system of banking. The Bank was allowed to lend its capital twice - once to the government and once to its new customers.

Over the years the deal has become much sweeter for the banks. In the early years of the 20th century, federally chartered U.S. banks were required to have a gold reserve equal to 25 percent of their deposits. State chartered banks were subject to less restraint, and there were some shocking examples of excess.

With the introduction of central banks, the Federal Reserve System in the U.S. and the Bank of Canada north of the border, the system changed in form though not in substance. Private banks no longer printed their own banknotes, copies of which many of us have hidden away as mementos. These were phased out of circulation and replaced by a uniform, legal tender, currency.

In the U.S., Federal Reserve Notes became predominant, while in Canada the Bank of Canada was given a monopoly on the creation of legal tender paper money. With the transition came the requirement for private banks to keep cash, legal tender, as reserves against their deposits, instead of gold.

Consequently, when I was younger, the cash reserve requirement for Canadian banks was 8% which allowed them to lend the same money 12½ times. Today the cash reserve requirement in the U.S. is 3% for current accounts, 0% for saving accounts, and 0% for Eurodollar accounts. In Canada, the reserve requirement is 0%, period! You are lucky if your bank has half a cent in cash for every dollar you think you have in the bank.[3]

The only reason the banks can get away with this is because they know from experience that only a handful of depositors are likely to ask for cash at any one time. If for any reason depositors' confidence was shaken, and they began a "run" on the bank, they would be out of luck because their "money" doesn't exist in real form. Their only hope would be for the Bank of Canada to turn on the printing presses and buy the private bank's assets with cash created for that purpose.

It was Prime Minister Brian Mulroney who eliminated the requirement for Canadian banks to hold cash reserves. The Bank Act of 1991 phased them out. Little wonder that Mulroney is revered on Bay Street. He handed the private banks a gift of several billion dollars of taxpayer's money which we have to hand over every year in perpetuity. What we pay the banks in interest on the treasury bills and bonds that they bought with the cash that they no longer have to keep in reserve would have been enough to make up the shortfall in the health care system.

PRIVATE BANKS PRINT MONEY

The fact that private banks print money is extremely difficult for many of my friends to accept. They don't print banknotes any more, as I have already pointed out; instead they print "credit money" or "virtual money" on their computers. The way the system works is, as Galbraith said, so simple that the mind is repelled.

You want to borrow $35,000 to buy a new car. So you visit your friendly banker and ask for a loan. You will be asked for collateral – some stocks, bonds, a 2nd mortgage on your house or cottage or, if you are unable to supply any of these, the co-signature of a well-to-do friend or relative. When the collateral requirement is satisfied, you will be asked to sign a note for the principal amount with an agreed rate of interest.

When the paperwork is complete, and the note signed, your banker will make an entry on the bank's computer and, presto, a $35,000 credit will appear in your account which you can use to buy your car. The important point is that seconds earlier that money did not exist. It was created out of thin air – so to speak.

The bank employs a kind of double-entry bookkeeping where your note becomes an asset on the bank's books, and your deposit is a liability for the bank. Their profit comes from the difference between the low rate of interest, if any, you would be paid on your deposit if you didn't spend the money immediately, and the much higher rate you would be obliged to pay on your note.

One of the most widely held myths about banking is that they are simply financial intermediaries, and lend you today the money that I or someone else deposited yesterday. That *myth* is far from the truth. They are financial intermediaries, but that isn't all. They also create new money every time they make a new loan – or destroy money when they cancel one.

The reason banking is such a profitable scam is due to their high leverage. When the requirement for cash reserves was abolished the Bank Act imposed a new system. Canadian banks are not allowed to own assets in excess of twenty times their paid up capital. At least that is what the law says, although anyone who examines the banks' annual statements will know that they have found ingenious means of stretching that limit. The new system, which is called "capital adequacy" is quite inferior to the necessity for cash reserves – the system to which Canada must return if it is going to achieve its destiny.

PRINTING MONEY PROVIDES POWER AND PROFIT

The fight over who should print the money, the state, on behalf of all the people, or the private banks in their own interests and those of their preferred customers, has been going on for centuries. Occasionally the state has won a round as was the case when President Abraham Lincoln printed money to help pay for the U.S. Civil War. It is widely believed that his experiment with government-created money (GCM) was the reason he was murdered.

Then there have been cases like war-time when the state intervened massively. That is how Canada escaped the Great Depression and helped finance World War II. In 1938 there were no jobs in Canada. None. Then in 1939 the war came along and pretty soon everyone was working – in the Armed Forces, building factories and making munitions.

You might wonder how this was financed. Simple. The Bank of Canada printed money and bought Government of Canada bonds with it. The government paid the Bank of Canada interest on the bonds but the Bank gave it back to the government in the form of dividends. In effect it was an interest-free loan – just the cost of administration deducted.

Meanwhile, the government spent the money into circulation to pay for the factories, the munitions and the salaries of the soldiers, sailors and airmen. The cash wound up in the private banks where it became what the economists called high powered money – the "cash reserves" which allowed the banks to create credit money to help finance new factories and to lend to people to buy Victory bonds.

In effect, the money-creation function was shared between the government, through the Bank of Canada, and the private banks. That was the system that worked so well in wartime and the early post-war years. It helped finance the post-war infrastructure including the St. Lawrence Seaway, the Trans Canada Highway, our great new airports and, it helped lay the foundation of our social security net. It was the system that gave Canada the best 25 years of the twentieth century.

Alas, the post-war prosperity was too good to last. Some economics professor had to come along and spoil everything. That professor, as I pointed out earlier, was Milton Friedman and his Chicago gang. They became accessories to the biggest heist in history. Although Friedman has recently admitted that his monetary mathematics was in error,[4] he has not yet recanted on the most damaging of his recommendations which was to get governments out of the money-creation function and let the private banks print nearly all of it.

Remember that banks are unique amongst commercial institutions in that they are the only corporations with licenses to print money. The patent for new money creation is owned by the federal parliament on behalf of the Canadian people. But for reasons which have more to do with historical precedent than any kind of logic, parliament has licensed its patent to privately owned commercial banks through Charters issued under the Bank Act.

To the extent that there is any logic in allowing private banks to create any money it is that they will ration it more fairly and wisely than government would. Their branch managers have been well positioned to get to know the farmers, business people and small entrepreneurs in need of financial assistance and to determine their credit worthiness. Even then, the banks were often unreasonable in their demands for collateral, and merciless in their treatment of borrowers in default.

The case for the banks was eroded when greed overwhelmed them. They got tired of the work involved in servicing their small customers, the ones who create the jobs, and turned their attention increasingly to wholesale, large-loan banking. This included leveraged buyouts which resulted in bidding up the price of assets (inflation) and then the elimination of redundant personnel – the necessity to become mean and lean (higher unemployment).

This shift in strategy by the banks seriously undermined the public trust aspect of their charters. Deals that were profitable to them were often contrary to the public interest. Wholesale banking also introduced a double standard. Loans to high-flying real estate operators were not collateralized to the extent small business loans had been. Furthermore, loans to Third World countries were not collateralized at all. So the banks' ability to act fairly and wisely, implicit in their charters, was exposed as largely myth.

Where the logic of parliament allowing private corporations to create money breaks down completely, however, is when the federal government allows the banks to print money to buy federal bonds and then acts as a collection agency for the banks to make sure that we, the taxpayers, pay interest on that money – perhaps in perpetuity, if the present system persists.

It would be a little less painful if parliament imposed a healthy royalty for the use of the people's money-creation patent. But the license, which has to be the most lucrative of all monetary windfalls, is issued without a royalty provision! Worse, the federal government, which still has the right to use its own patent, stubbornly refuses to do so. Can you think of anything more ridiculous?

Why would any government in its right mind borrow money from private banks, and pay 5 or 6 percent interest on the loans, when it could borrow the same amount of money from its own bank at a net cost of less than 1 percent? The word ridiculous is far too mild. It is gross incompetence. Yet our government has been doing that since Milton Friedman filled the minds of our senior bankers and public servants with monetary malignancy.

And the same curse has spread from country-to-country like the global plague it has become. Governments, which own the right, are forbidden to print money to help finance health care and education. Only private banks, which have been granted the privilege, are allowed to print money. Governments, to meet any shortfall from time to time, have to borrow from the voracious entities that were born of their own midwifery and go deeper into debt – witness the balance sheets of all the world's economies. It is a kind of perpetual slavery with the banks calling the shots and the people paying taxes to service the debt.

Little wonder that the banks want to play monopoly, both nationally and internationally. And they are likely to get away with it if the record of the Canadian parliament is a reliable precedent. It never says "no" to the banks for very long. There is an occasional pause to provide time to digest previous acquisitions; but then the juggernaut, with its inevitable propaganda about bigger "being in the public interest," begins again.

It is a short-sighted policy, of course. If additions to the money supply are not used to finance the entrepreneurs who create the jobs for workers who pay taxes to service the debt, where will we wind up as a society? In debt, of course, and with so much of our money going for interest that there isn't enough for health and education. Like now, for example, but with even worse to come.

The rest of the world, and especially its poor parts, suffers from this same plague of global financial monopolization. Which is why we should all pay closer attention to what the banks do, and what they are up to.

CHAPTER 8

THE BANKS PLAY MONOPOLY

"The manufacturing process to make money consists of making an entry in a book. That is all."

Graham Towers
First Governor of the Bank of Canada

The history of banking has been one of increased power and profitability. There have been setbacks, of course, like the Great Depression when hundreds of U.S. banks went bankrupt because they didn't have the cash to meet their depositors' demands. Canadian banks fared better due to their extensive branch systems and their ruthless foreclosures.

World War II bailed out the survivors and the tremendous infusion of new cash gave all the players in the financial system a new lease on life. Canadian banks were no exception. The economy grew rapidly, and so did the banks. Prosperity had returned, big time.

You would think that when the banks had such a good thing going for them that they would have been content. But that was not the case. Every time the Bank Act was reviewed, and their charters renewed, they asked for more. Profitability was the name of the game and each time they extended their tentacles into other people's businesses, competition was reduced and the banks' relentless drive toward monopolizing the financial services sector advanced one more step.

At one time there were "four pillars" of the financial world – banks, trust companies, securities dealers and insurance companies. The banks have effectively bulldozed two of the three pillars – trust companies and securities dealers – to the point where all serious competition has been effectively eliminated. They are now working on the fourth pillar, the insurance companies, and only an unmistakable vote of disapproval from the government will prevent the near total consolidation of the financial services industry under the banks' umbrella.

To accomplish their ends, the banks have used every tactic and argument their high-priced paid help could dream up. A number of years ago, when the banks were not allowed to make consumer loans, the Bank of Nova Scotia began to defy the law while counting on its propaganda offensive to the effect that it would save consumers money. The gamble paid off and the restriction on consumer loans was lifted. Most of the consumer loan companies have since disappeared.

When Jacques Parizeau, then finance minister in the Liberal government in Québec, decided to play Québec interests against those of Ontario by allowing provincially chartered deposit-taking institutions to buy into brokerage firms, he set off a chain of events which he did not envisage. The threat of losing business was the wedge needed to pry loose more favourable conditions from Ontario regulators who dropped the rule limiting banks to 10% ownership of a brokerage firm.

The Toronto-Dominion Bank had provided the thin edge of the wedge with its Green Line Service which was restricted at the outset, but was soon liberated as the barriers fell and the race was on. Royal Bank bought Dominion Securities, the Bank of Montreal bought Nesbitt Thomson, the CIBC bought Wood Gundy, the Bank of Nova Scotia acquired McLeod Young Weir and the National Bank swallowed Levésque-Beaubien, the largest Québec-based dealer.

These takeovers constituted one of the biggest consolidations of power and influence in the history of Canadian financial institutions. It also posed a new dilemma for banks owning a broker. How could it deal at arms length with its subsidiary which was borrowing money to buy stocks or to float new share issues? And would it be influenced in any way in making credit available to customers wishing to buy shares being peddled by a subsidiary?

The answer, we were told, was Chinese walls. One branch of the conglomerate would be forbidden to whisper, let alone speak of, information that would be of advantage or disadvantage to its subsidiary, and this prohibition would apply in both directions.

It was the joke of the century. Within weeks of the ink being dry on the Royal Bank takeover of Dominion Securities I had a call from a retail salesperson. The Royal Bank quarterly statement would be coming out in a few days, I was informed. The results would be excellent and it was anticipated that the market value of Royal Bank stock would rise. I was appalled that the myth of inter-branch secrecy would be stripped bare so quickly. As a matter of principle I didn't buy any Royal Bank stock, but any moral gain was at a financial cost because the results were good and the price did go up.

THE COUP OF 1991

The banks were not satisfied with gobbling up most of the major securities dealers. They wanted more. So in advance of the 1991 revision of the Bank Act they lobbied ferociously in favour of the idea of "one-stop financial shopping" under which, presumably, anyone in the financial services business could own anything. Equally insidious, they argued that the trust companies had an advantage because they were not required to maintain cash reserves against their deposits. What the banks wanted was a "level playing field."

That sounds like a "tilt" if ever I heard one. There is no such thing as a level-playing field when you are playing against the banks. It is interesting that the banks didn't argue that the trusts and other deposit-taking institutions should be required to maintain cash reserves. The banks wanted them eliminated altogether, after re-naming them a "tax on the banks."

Well, it must have been Christmas in bankland. Brian Mulroney's finance minister, Michael Wilson, introduced a bill removing the rules that kept the banks from majority ownership of trust companies and out of the insurance game. They were not allowed to sell insurance over the counter, in their branches, but they were allowed to buy trust and insurance companies.

Another pot of gold was the total elimination, over a three-year period, of the cash reserve requirement. As I mentioned in the previous chapter, this bonanza was worth billions to the banks, and while the whole gift package was being wrapped in legislative cellophane with a pretty ribbon and the bow tied, members of parliament slept. This is not surprising for government backbenchers who open their mouths at considerable risk; but one wonders what kind of gas was required to muzzle the then Liberal opposition to such a degree that one would have thought that they were in a state of winter hibernation.

The removal of statutory reserve requirements effective July, 1994, provided an incentive for the banks to reduce their note holdings. The proportion of currency (GCM) in circulation held by chartered banks has thus declined from nearly 17% in 1991, to less than 9% in 2003.[1] The reduced need for cash – the banks truck it back and forth between branches overnight in order to keep inventories low – means less seigniorage (profit) for the Crown (taxpayers). It is one more way of diverting money from the public coffers to bank tills. Even federal officials are concerned that the explosive increase in the use of credit cards, debit cards and cash cards will mean an even further loss of seigniorage.

You have already guessed the banks' next move in this decades-long monopoly game. They rescued the struggling trust companies, whose earlier advantage they considered so unfair, by buying them. In doing so they virtually eliminated the modest competition the trust companies had provided with their longer hours, marginally higher interest rates paid on deposits, split level mortgages and flexible Guaranteed Investment certificates. After the purchase of National Trust by the Bank of Nova Scotia, and then Canada Trust by Toronto Dominion, competition from that former pillar of the financial system had been eliminated.

The impact of all this consolidation is almost beyond comprehension. Slowly but surely the banks have been getting into other people's businesses. First they infiltrate, like the camel getting its head into the tent, and then they take over. The big five now own more than 400 subsidiaries and the list is growing. In addition to financial services they are now involved in energy, aviation, leasing, insurance and other activities.

Their success is reflected in their enormous profits and there is some suspicion that even these are understated due to write-offs of acquisition costs and related charges. Curiously, some of their subsidiaries are located in the Cayman Islands, Guernsey and other "tax havens." One wonders just what role these subsidiaries play and whether their existence reduces federal tax revenues in any way. I thought of this when I read that CIBC had earned $1.69 billion in 2001 but reported paying just $92 million in income taxes – an effective rate of just 5 percent when none of the other banks paid less than 27 percent.[2] It is a virtual certainty that deregulation has been good for the banks but less so for taxpayers at large.

THE FINAL PUSH

There are a few small bones that banks have been denied until now and a cynic might be forgiven for suspecting this is largely for cosmetic political purposes. The banks have been denied access to the car leasing business, and are still not allowed to sell insurance over the counter, although they can own insurance companies. Why they should be allowed to do either heaven only knows. Corporations that have licenses to print money should not be allowed to compete with companies that do not. It is not a level playing field by any stretch of the imagination.

Now, however, the banks have bigger fish to fry – at least some of them do. For several years the biggest of the banks have sought the right to merge so they will become even bigger. They claim that they are too small to be major players in the globalized banking arena of the future.

For many years the Bank Act did not facilitate mergers due to the 10% rule which prohibited any one person from owning more than 10% of the shares of any Schedule I bank. This rule, according to Charles Baillie, former chairman of the Toronto-Dominion Bank, was put in place in the 1960s because Chase Manhattan of New York wanted to buy his bank. Recently, as a result of intense lobbying, that 10% limit has been increased to 20 percent.

When the merger craze began in 1996 and 1997, the TD did not support the bigger banks initiative. According to Baillie, a smaller bank is a better bank. "In today's world you succeed by being smarter, by having a good strategy and executing it well. Size is not a strategy. It's a statistic." Baillie was speaking to the annual meeting of his bank in January, 1997, in an attempt to reassure his employees who suspected that the TD would be the first takeover target in a deregulated market, and that their jobs would be in jeopardy.

My, what a difference a few years makes. Not only did TD acquire Canada Trust, a move that our moribund Competition Bureau should have disallowed, but Baillie became a total convert to the "bigger is better" school of corporate thinking. It is like one of the new viruses spreading around the world – one for which civilized society has not yet found an effective cure.

A Royal Bank study in 1996 observed that Canadian banks had slipped in their world ranking, and none were included in the top 50 – largely because Japanese banks had grown rapidly in the previous 20 years. But anyone who has studied Japanese banks knows that they had a certain puff ball quality which had to be taken into account for a proper evaluation. Since that study was done, most Japanese banks have fallen on hard times and, as usual, the taxpayers have had to bail them out to the tune of countless billions. Since 1996, the Royal Bank has crept into 48th place worldwide.[3]

But a more relevant question is how Canadian banks rank in North America. All five major banks rank in the top fifteen.[4] That, in my opinion, is big enough. Obviously the banks don't agree. They have been waging a propaganda war to convince Canadians that bank mergers are necessary if we are to play in the major league, and that mergers are inevitable in the kind of world in which we live.

It is interesting to note, when reading old newspaper clippings, that every time the Bank Act comes up for review, and the banks call for change "in the public interest," that we are subject to a massive propaganda campaign. The Canadian Bankers Association launches an all-out lobbying effort. The financial papers are willing allies.

In the first round of merger-mania, the *Financial Post* was lead batter with its editorial of April 12, 1996, "Canadian banks need size to compete internationally," it said: "Canada's banks are only minnows in the world fish pond. The biggest bank in the world is Japan's newly-merged Bank of Tokyo-Mitsubishi Ltd. with assets of $U.S. 86-billion; that's five times bigger than any Canadian bank."[5] This was followed up a few days later in the Dominion Bond Rating Service Ltd.'s banking industry review, lauding banks, and saying they face consolidation because there are too many for the size of the Canadian market. The DBRS's wisdom was duly reported in both the *Financial Post* and the *Globe and Mail* on April 26, 1996.

In October, 1996, the then Bank of Montreal chief, Matthew Barrett, called on Ottawa to allow mergers among the Big Six so they could meet competition over the next decade. He was honest enough to admit that, "It is inescapable, if there are mergers, there will be some adjustments." Analysts had predicted up to 10,000 jobs could be lost if two of the big banks merge.[6] The Canadian banks claimed that they were not big enough to compete internationally; but when it came to propaganda they were world class.

On Friday, June 20, 1997, the *Globe and Mail* ran a full page lead editorial entitled "Carve up the sacred cow of bank ownership," in which it opined that the time had come to end the 10% limitation on bank ownership in order to facilitate mergers and the potential takeover by foreigners. It acknowledged, however, that there could be negative consequences for the Canadian economy if the whole industry were foreign controlled.[7]

A few days later the Bank of Montreal released a 69-page document entitled "Policy Alternatives for Canadian Financial Services" as its contribution to the Task Force set up by the Minister of Finance to advise the government on changes required in the financial services industry. It plumped for further deregulation of the industry, an end to the prohibition against car leasing and over the counter insurance sales by the banks and, most significant of all, "the 10% limit on shareholdings by any single interest should be amended to allow for the takeover of domestic banks by widely held foreign institutions."[8]

Wow! At least you have to give the Bank of Montreal high marks for honesty in calling a spade a spade. Already you can sense the cards being passed back and forth under the table in this high stakes poker game. Still the next play took many by surprise. "Banks drop $40 billion bombshell," read the front page headline in the *Globe and Mail*; "Surprise megamerger plan by Royal and Bank of Montreal sets stage for showdown over federal approval."[9]

The result of that showdown was not what the banks were hoping for. They had presented their plan as a *fait accompli* but without the courtesy of advising the government and the Minister of Finance, Paul Martin, that it was coming. They just acted as if they owned the country, which they more or less do, but neither governments, which still exercise some power, nor ordinary bank customers like having their noses rubbed into their relative insignificance. The banks had arrogantly ignored a cardinal rule of politics.

The omission cost them dearly. The government was furious. Paul Martin was furious. Back-bench Members of Parliament were furious. Liberal backbenchers, in particular, told Martin that if he approved the deal he could forget about his wish to become leader of the Liberal Party. There was power in those words, so Martin told the banks the deal was off, and parliament would have to study the question of the public interest before any proposal could be re-visited. So the millions the banks had spent on their clandestine plans went down the sink.

But that was then, and now is now; and a lot of water has gone under the proverbial bridge. The propaganda war in favour of deregulation and consolidation of the financial services industry has continued unabated. Paul Martin was given time off from his cabinet duties to concentrate his efforts on the Liberal leadership race. John Manley took over as finance minister and quite obviously concluded that the time had come to review both the situation and the process.

"Manley stokes merger hopes" read the headline in the *Globe's* Report on Business, on October 25, 2002.[10] "Manley bids to restart bank mergers debate; Bankers welcome study on mergers," the *Toronto Star* reported the same day.[11] "The door to re-examine the mergers was already open because of the policy adopted a year ago. It's unfinished business,"[12] Manley was quoted as saying.

The Finance Minister asked two parliamentary committees, the Senate Committee on Banking, Trade and Commerce, and the House of Commons Standing Committee on Finance, to study all the usual questions about regional access to quality financial services, the needs of small business, Canada's international competitiveness and how to ease the pain for the people who would inevitably lose their jobs as a result. In effect they were asked to clarify the review process. Such a monumental event as bank mergers would be easier for the public to swallow if they felt they had been consulted and the very real questions concerning "the public interest" had been addressed and provided for.

Although Manley had portrayed his letter to the two parliamentary committees as basic housekeeping, banks and investors read it as a signal that the political climate was at long last more favourable for mergers. Shares of Scotiabank shot up 2.9%, those of CIBC increased by 2.9%, while the price of Bank of Montreal stock jumped by 3.4 percent.

Clearly the market believed that the green light had just been switched on. "In Manley's request," opined the *Toronto Star*, "the markets clearly saw an attempt to narrow the scope for the way in which the public interest is defined. That is something the banks have wanted."[13]

And that is what the two parliamentary committees immediately set out to do, with what some of us considered as almost indecent haste. But the banks, at least two of them, having either learned nothing from previous experience, or having concluded that the minister was prepared to act at once, cooked up a deal without bothering to wait to hear what the public and the committees might have to say.

"Banks were set to seal merger," screamed the headline on the front page of the *Globe and Mail*. "The Bank of Nova Scotia and Bank of Montreal were just two weeks away from announcing a block-buster merger that would have created Canada's largest bank when the Prime Minister's office effectively killed the bid ..."[14]   People involved in the negotiations said that the Bank of Montreal and Scotiabank were so close to finalizing the terms of the deal that they had already agreed on the valuations for their respective stocks.

Good for the Prime Minister. Whether he was guarding the principle of parliamentary integrity, or giving his lieutenant a gentle rap over the knuckles only the two of them know. But killing the deal, and convincing the banks that no mergers will be approved before the next election, expected in 2004, has provided some much needed time for sober second thoughts concerning one of the half dozen most important decisions facing Canada today.

SOBER SECOND THOUGHTS

If we were expecting sober second thoughts from the Senate Committee on Banking, Trade and Commerce, allegedly the function that justifies the continued existence of that august chamber, we certainly didn't get it. Its report was signed by Senator E. Leo Kolber, chair, and deputy chair Senator David Tkachuk, who said on the CBC program "As It Happens" that bank mergers "were in the public interest." Period! He made it sound as thought the report had been written by one of the banks' chief executive officers. Canada's economy would be strengthened by having just three large banks.

Furthermore, the politicians should butt out of the decision making process. Proposals for bank mergers should be reviewed and approved by the Competition Bureau and the Office of the Superintendent of Financial Institutions. If the Minister of Finance chose to reject their recommendation, he would have to justify the decision before parliament.

Well, that is certainly in line with the world trend of transferring sovereignty and power from elected representatives to unelected, unaccountable bureaucrats. It is a frightening trend. It is especially frightening to think that the Competition Bureau would be the critical component of the decision-making apparatus. The Bureau is attached to the Department of Trade which is one of the three government departments most responsible for selling Canada down the river. Worse, the current head of the Bureau has been deeply involved in the process and is one of a handful of Canadians I would least trust to protect the public interest.

The Commons committee report was more muted in language, if not in ultimate intent. The document, tabled by committee chair Sue Barnes, MP, said merger proposals must be reviewed by the Competition Bureau, the Office of the Superintendent of Financial Institutions (OSFI) and the Commons Finance Committee, with the final decision still in the hands of the Minister of Finance.

The report was criticized for its lack of clarity. Even the vice-chairman, Nick Discepola, Liberal MP for the Québec riding of Vaudreuil-Soulanges, dismissed the report as "non-committal." That is consistent with the whole debate, however, and the softening up of resistance in advance of action being taken.

Increasingly, the public interest is being redefined in a way that coincides with the interests of the biggest banks. The brainwashing is virtually complete and no one is exposing the reality of the booby-trap that is being set for us.

Bank mergers are not in the public interest! The best advice Ottawa has received on this subject came from TD Bank's new CEO Edmund Clark who said: "Put no limit on mergers or ban all."[15] Faced with this choice, there is no contest. There should be no mergers and, for the sake of clarity, the banks should be given the message clearly so they can get on with more constructive plans.

Consider the alternative. With no limits, the initial consolidation would be to three. But that wouldn't satisfy them, as their record in eliminating competition clearly shows. They would contrive to make it two. If, of course, one of the big three didn't wind up in foreign hands in the meantime.

Lloyd Atkinson, chief investment officer at Perigee Investment Counsel Inc., and former chief economist at the Bank of Montreal, described Finance Minister John Manley's letter to the two parliamentary committees as a "trial balloon" that will likely trigger a series of events in the governance of Canadian banks. Those events will include, within four or five years, the first takeover of a Canadian bank by a foreign institution.[16]

There are three principal reasons for saying no to bank mergers. They don't need to do it; they don't deserve the windfall that would accrue to the few; and allowing mergers to take place would be a Canadian stamp of approval to the greed-driven globalization of financial services which is bad for the world and bad for Canada. Let's look at these three in reverse order.

As Joseph Stiglitz, former chief economist of the World Bank, pointed out in his book *Globalization and its Discontents*, it was unrestricted capital movements, forced on reluctant countries by the U.S. Treasury Department, which were largely responsible for the East Asia meltdown. The social and economic damage reached astronomical proportions. The spillover cost even Canada tens of millions of dollars as world commodity prices tanked.

The whole world system is headed in the wrong direction – one of instability and unpredictability. The future of the world depends on smaller banks and smaller companies – something that comes closer to a genuine market system. The insatiable greed of the financial institutions can only be met by financing monopoly economics – the elimination of competition on a global scale. And with it, the elimination of jobs.

Numerous experiments have shown that the only hope for millions of people in poor countries is microbanking – the ability of individuals to borrow a hundred dollars or so to set themselves up in a business that will give them a livelihood and independence from a fate determined by the whims of others.

Canadian entrepreneurs need somewhat larger loans but for the same reasons. I know whereof I speak. As a young entrepreneur I had to get bank assistance to help finance the fledgling building business I had invested in. And I had to shop around. Without competition it would have been game over before the end of the first inning. With bank assistance, and a lot of hard work, the company became innovative, eventually profitable, and created many jobs and significant wealth.

The opportunity for young Canadians to succeed, as thousands of my generation did, vanishes for some every time a bank branch is closed. You can't borrow $10,000 from an ATM. That is the reason that branch closures are really anti-Canadian. It is the banks' way of saying "we don't really care about small Canadian entrepreneurs. They are far too much of a nuisance to justify either the work or the risk involved."

Instead of financing small entrepreneurs the banks have favoured wholesale banking including mergers and leveraged buyouts. These inevitably result in fewer jobs, especially in middle management. People who have worked for a company for years or decades suddenly find themselves out on the street with nothing more than a golden handshake as a memento.

Worse, Canadian banks have been financing the sale of Canadian companies to foreigners. Our Trade Department lauds the advantages of direct foreign investment. But the sale of existing Canadian companies to foreigners is just a give away when part or all of the purchase price is a loan from Canadian banks. Not only is our money supply diluted in the process, but we inherit the privilege of paying out profits to the new foreign owners, in perpetuity.

To add injury to insult, the head offices move out, the best decision making jobs go with the head offices and young Canadians aspiring to the top jobs have to leave Canada.

Furthermore, foreign-owned companies pay less tax in Canada than domestically owned companies so we have to cut back public services or ante up the difference in revenue. In effect, Canadian banks have been nation-wreckers *par excellence*.

With a record like this the banks deserve no sympathy for their latest efforts to disadvantage Canadians even further. Any merger will result in job losses in the order of 10,000 based on studies for the first proposed mergers in 1997-8. So if Peter Godsoe, CEO of Scotiabank, can be taken seriously when he says bank mergers at the cost of jobs won't fly – a concern that is open to serious doubt in view of his spotty record on the question of mergers – no merger will fly. Not only would they result in job losses, both competition and service would be further eroded.

Finally, the banks don't need to merge! Look at one of the possible couples. Royal Bank net income before taxes increased from $63 million in 1992 to $4.421 billion in 2002.[17] Not bad, eh? The junior partner, Bank of Montreal, increased its net income before taxes from $1.127 billion in 1992 to $2.009 billion in 2002,[18] which was a bad year for BMO. There appears to be no need to pass the hat and take up a collection for the banks.

I was intrigued by a front page article in the *Globe and Mail* of May 31, 2003. "RBC to push harder into U.S.; CEO cites no merger climate in Canada," it was titled. 'Certainly I think it's more clear to us that we're probably looking down the road a couple of years as opposed to the near term,' Mr. Nixon said of the likely timetable for mergers. 'If that is the case, I think we will start to see an acceleration, or certainly from our perspective, an ability to look at more aggressively investing in our platform in the U.S., particularly in the personal and commercial banking businesses in the Southeast.'"[19]

Can you find the missing word in that business plan? Could it be Canada? And is this the same Gordon Nixon who not long ago was decrying the "hollowing out" of Canadian industry? I wonder why? I think we will have to buy him a mirror for his birthday so he will be able to see the source of the problem.

I remember Sue Barnes, MP, Chair of the Commons Committee on Finance, saying that parliament shouldn't attempt to micromanage the banks. Of course it shouldn't. But when banks are constantly creating money to dilute the Canadian money supply, citizens have an absolute right to know the purpose of the dilution and whether it's in Canada's best interest or someone else's.

I am not willing to see the value of my money diluted to provide "personal and commercial" banking (read jobs) in the U.S. until those needs in Canada have been adequately met – which, as of now, they have not.

One thing is absolutely clear. Canadian banks do not need to merge to expand their operations in the U.S. and elsewhere. They have already invested billions outside the country, and lost a fair bit of it. But not to worry, they have used their Canadian operations and tax write-offs to cover their losses.

If you have concluded that I am opposed to further consolidation of Canada's financial services industry you have read me correctly. The banks have really stuck it to us, and they need to make amends. The problems they have caused in this country are not unlike those created by big international banks in other parts of the world. Somehow, somewhere, someday, the carnage will have to stop.

CHAPTER 9

MULRONEY'S SIZZLE IS A FIZZLE

"You can fool some of the people all of the time, and all of the people some of the time, but you cannot fool all of the people all of the time."

Abraham Lincoln

As I watched a TV clip of Brian Mulroney singing his own praises at the PC convention in Toronto at the end of May, 2003, I was reminded of an earlier newspaper article I had seen entitled "Praise for free trade is long overdue, Mulroney declares." "Former Prime Minister Brian Mulroney says it's about time his former political foes in the Liberal and Alliance parties started singing the praises of free trade,"[1] the article began.

"Not so," I remember thinking when I read the article. "It's time they started to do some hard research and learn for themselves that the Free Trade Agreement and the North American Free Trade Agreement, about which Mulroney boasts, have been a disaster for Canada. So much so that unless the treaties are abrogated there will be no Canada in a decade or two."

Of these two diametrically opposite views, Mulroney's is the one which is currently most popular. An Ipsos-Reid poll released on June 8, 2003 indicated that 70 percent of respondents supported NAFTA, though a bare majority – 51 percent – said the deal has benefited Canada. This is a significant increase since January, 2001, when 64 percent were in support and only 40 percent thought it had benefited this country.[2]

102

You will wonder, of course, why my strongly held position is so different from the public consensus. The answer, in a nutshell, is that the average person on the street only knows what he or she has been told. Story after story in the newspapers, and on radio and TV, have referred to the large increase in trade between Canada and the U.S. since the FTA was signed, and sometimes provide the statistics to prove it.

The facts show that there has been a big increase in cross-border trade. That is the truth. But, as in so many other cases, it is only part of the truth and, in my opinion, only the most superficial aspect of it. Inevitably the "pro-free trade" stories will fail to analyze how much of the increase in trade would have occurred without the FTA. Nor do they mention the many negative aspects of the FTA and NAFTA which exceed the benefits.

Let's look first at the increase in exports and imports and put the gains and losses in some reasonable perspective.

EXPORTS AND IMPORTS

Canada's biggest gains in exports to the U.S. since the FTA was signed have been in automobiles and auto parts, energy and agricultural products. In all three cases the connection to the FTA, if any, has been minimal. In the case of automobiles, the increase has been largely attributable to the Auto Pact which represented Canadian "protectionism" at its best and most successful. This advantage was amplified, of course, by the dramatic fall in the relative value of the Canadian dollar. Chart No. 1 tells the story.

These figures are bloated by more than $12 billion due to double accounting. Car parts are counted as imports or exports as they cross the border to be installed in a car, and counted a second time when the completed car is subsequently shipped back across the same border.

The most dramatic increase in Canadian exports to the U.S. has been energy – electricity, crude oil and natural gas. This is due to the almost insatiable demand for energy south of the border. Exports will continue to rise with or without NAFTA. Indeed, a number of U.S. officials have expressed the view that Canada will not have sufficient natural gas to meet U.S. demand.   Chart No. 2 shows the trend which reflects higher prices as well as increased volume.

Chart No. 1
Automotive Trade with U.S.

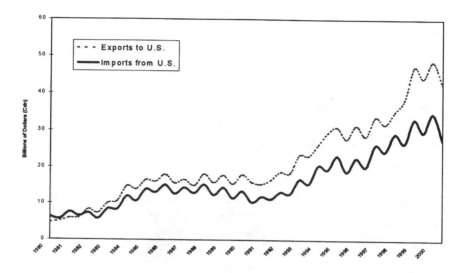

Chart No. 2
Energy Exports to U.S.

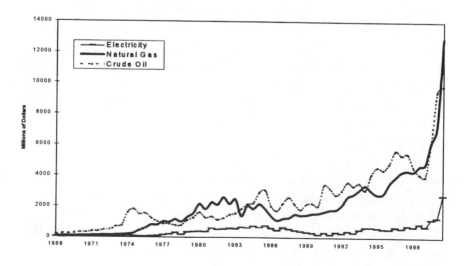

A third area in which phenomenal growth in exports has occurred is agriculture. Unfortunately, however, the benefits have bypassed both farmers and consumers. This is the story of the FTA and NAFTA. A small minority have profited handsomely while the vast majority are as bad or worse off than they were before. The National Farmers Union has prepared a compendium which illuminates the negative aspects of "free trade." I am reproducing much of it here because it is information everyone should see and think about. The figures shown are in current dollars – not adjusted for inflation.

	1988	**2002**
Canadian agri-food exports	**$10.9 billion**	**$28.2 billion**

Canadian farmers have been extremely successful in increasing exports, in gaining "access" to foreign markets. We have nearly tripled agri-food exports since 1988 and exports are seven times higher than in 1975.

Realized net farm income	**$3.9 billion**	**$4.1 billion**

These figures are not adjusted for inflation. If we adjust for inflation, net farm income is down 24%.

Farm debt	**$22.5 billion**	**$44.2 billion**

Farm debt has doubled since we implemented the Canada-U.S. Free Trade Agreement. Today, interest on the debt nearly equals Canadian net farm income. The banks are taking nearly as much from our farms as the families who own those farms are earning.

Wheat: farmgate price	**$4.93/bushel**	**$4.48/bushel**

Prices are for #1 Canadian Western Red Spring wheat, 11.5% protein, Saskatoon net (freight and elevator tariffs subtracted). See the note on the Two-Price Wheat program in the section on bread, below.

Bread: grocery store price	**$1.12/loaf**	**$1.46/loaf**

In 1988, Canada still had a Two-Price Wheat (TPW) program. That program set a price for wheat used in Canada that was higher but more stable than the world price. In 1988, Canadian millers were making $1.12 bread out of $7.00 (domestic-price) wheat. Today, they make $1.46 bread out of $4.48 wheat. The TPW program put up to $12,000 per year into the pocket of an average-size wheat producer. The bread price data cited here seems to indicate that the TPW program cost consumers nothing. <u>The program was cancelled in 1988 in anticipation that it would violate the then-pending Canada-U.S. Free Trade Agreement.</u>

	1988	2002
Grain Handling: # of farmer-owned co-ops	**4**	**0**

In 1988, four farmer-owned co-ops handled the vast majority of western grain (the Saskatchewan, Alberta, and Manitoba Pools and United Grain Growers). Today, Agricore United (formerly Manitoba and Alberta Pools and United Grain Growers, and with significant ownership by U.S.-based Archer Daniels Midland), Saskatchewan Wheat Pool (a former farmer-owned co-op that may soon be controlled by a U.S.-based corporation such as ConAgra), and Cargill have 75% of western grain-handling capacity.

| **Flour mills: Canadian ownership** | **50% of cap.** | **21% of cap.** |

One U.S.-based transnational, Archer Daniels Midland (ADM), owns 47% of Canadian flour milling capacity. ADM owned 0% in the mid-1980s, before the Canada-U.S. Free Trade Agreement.

| **Malt plants: Canadian ownership** | **95% of cap.** | **12% of cap.** |

Canada's malt capacity is predominantly owned by foreign-based transnationals such as ConAgra, Cargill, Rahr Malting, and Archer Daniels Midland.

| **Empl. in agri-food processing** | **277,300 jobs** | **274,900 jobs** |

Politicians blithely predicted that "Free Trade" and the end of the Crow would dramatically increase the number of Canadian jobs in value-added food processing, thus providing employment for rural residents.

| **Freight rates** (Saskatoon example) | **$7.15/tonne** | **$35.68/tonne** |

When the federal government took the Crow Benefit from farmers in 1995, it pointed to the need to comply with the then-new World Trade Organization (WTO) Agreement on Agriculture.

| **Fertilizer price** (anhydrous ammonia) | **$374/tonne** | **$539/tonne** |

Trade agreements and globalization have triggered waves of agribusiness mergers, dramatically decreasing competition between the dominant corporations and increasing their market power. Canada's dominant fertilizer manufacturers have grown exponentially. Terra Industries, Agrium, and Potash Corporation of Saskatchewan are all eight to twelve times larger than they were ten years ago.

| **Number of farmers in Canada** | **293,089** | **246,923** |

In the half-generation since Canada signed the Canada-U.S. Free Trade Agreement, corporate and government policies have forced 16% of our farmers off the land. In just the past five years (1996 to 2001), we have lost 11% of our family farms.

	1988	**2002**
Diesel fuel price (Alberta example)	25.0c/litre	33.5c/litre

Canada's leading fuel refiners/retailers – Shell Canada, Petro-Canada, and Imperial Oil – recorded record profits in 2000 and 2001. Exxon owns 70% of Imperial Oil. Royal Dutch Shell owns 78% of Shell Canada. Petro-Canada is a widely-held, publicly-traded corporation (the Canadian government owns 20%). Fuel prices are higher in other Canadian provinces.

Number of major machinery companies	**6**	**3**

In 1988, a Canadian farmer could buy a medium-sized tractor from Ford/Versatile, White, Massey Ferguson, Case IH, John Deere, or Deutz/Allis Chalmers. Today, CNH (an amalgam of Case, International Harvester, Ford, NewHolland, Steiger, Versatile, and others) and John Deere dominate major machinery sales with annual sales of about $10 billion and $13 billion respectively. AGCO (Massey Ferguson, Heston, Gleaner, White) has sales of about $2.5 billion annually. [All figures in this paragraph are in U.S. $.)

Fed.Gov. spending on farm support	**$4.7 billion**	**$3.5 billion**

These figures are not adjusted for inflation. If we adjust for inflation, 2001/02 federal government "spending in support of agriculture" is at its sixth lowest level in 18 years. This low level of spending comes despite a grinding farm income crisis and weather-related production problems.

Dairy: % processed by farmer co-ops	**60%**	**35%**

Large corporations are consuming our farmer-owned dairy co-ops. Saputo Inc. (Québec-based; $3 billion revenues) took over Dairyworld Co-op in 2001. Parmalat (Italian-based; approximately $11 billion revenues) is also a major corporate player. The three largest processors handle 71% of Canada's milk: only one is a co-op.

Pork chops: grocery store price	**$6.88/kg**	**$9.54/kg**

Canadians are told that fewer and larger farms will result in "higher efficiency." The benefits of that efficiency are elusive, however. While corporate and government policies have reduced the number of Canadian hog farmers by 2/3, packers and retailers have increased grocery-store pork chop prices by 39%.

	1988	**2002**
Number of hog farmers	33,760	11,565

Of the farms that were raising hogs in 1988, corporate and government policies have since forced 66% out of production. Smithfield Foods, the world's largest producer/packer, will raise about 14 million hogs in North America this year and slaughter and pack about 20 million. Total Canadian production is about 26 million slaughtered hogs per year. Smithfield has packing plants and production contracts across Canada.

| **Hogs: farmgate price** | $1.44/kg | $1.46/kg |

While grocery-store pork chop prices are up 39%, farmgate prices are up only 2%. Seen another way, while hog farmers are still receiving about the same $1.44/kg, packers and retailers have increased their *margin* (between the price they pay to farmers and the price they charge consumers) by $2.64/kg.

| **Packing plant pay** (typ. starting wage) | $9.38/hr | $9.65/hr |

When adjusted for inflation, starting wages at many plants are down sharply. Packers are using their growing market power to push up prices to consumers, push down prices to farmers, and push down wages for workers. In the wake of the NAFTA, packers have argued that Canadian wages must be competitive with U.S. wages. U.S. wages, in turn, must be competitive with Mexican wages. Some Canadian packers, unable to attract workers, are bringing in workers from Mexico.[3]

Why isn't "Free Trade" working for farmers? "Farmers have doubled exports, and doubled them again; we've adopted new technologies, 'high-value' crops, and exotic livestock; we've poured billions of dollars of investment into our farms; and, together with governments, we've signed numerous trade agreements. Farmers have done everything recommended by free trade and globalization advocates. And the result is the worst farm income crisis since the 1930s. Why hasn't free trade yielded the predicted benefits for farmers?

"For farmers, so-called 'Free Trade' agreements do two things simultaneously:

- By removing tariffs, quotas, and duties, these agreements erase the economic borders between nations and force the world's one billion farmers into a single, hyper-competitive market.
- At the same time, these agreements facilitate waves of agribusiness mergers that nearly eliminate competition for these corporations.
- Economists agree: when competition increases – as it has for farmers – prices and profits decrease. And when competition decreases – as for agribusiness corporations – prices and profits *increase*. Thus trade agreements and globalization predictably decrease farmers' prices and profits and increase prices and profits for the dominant agribusiness corporations."[4]

The bottom line is that despite playing the game the global way, and achieving a huge increase in exports that "free trade" supporters boast about, Canadian farmers are no better off now than they were before the FTA, and many have been driven out of business by the transnational corporations. Chart No. 3 is a pictorial summary of the experience in agriculture. It is fair to say that the same chart really tells the story of Canada's experience under the FTA and NAFTA.

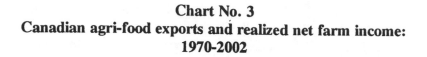

Chart No. 3
Canadian agri-food exports and realized net farm income:
1970-2002

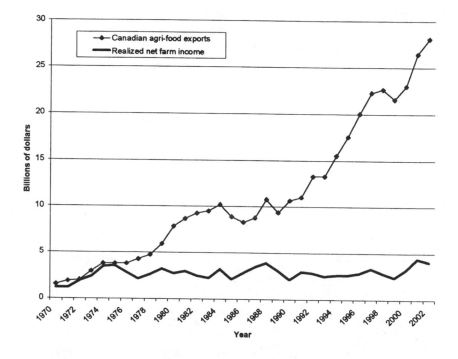

It is my firmly held belief that most of the increase in exports that has occurred since 1989 would have taken place in the absence of both the FTA and NAFTA. Furthermore I am convinced that the standard of living of the average Canadian would have been higher today in the absence of both treaties. Add to this the environmental damage we are suffering as a result, in addition to the very significant loss of control over our own affairs, and you have to ask yourself what in heaven's name Brian Mulroney and his negotiators were thinking about when they got us into this mess.

CANADIANS WERE DUPED

Canadians were duped into believing that the FTA was a trade agreement. I was naïve enough to believe it, because that is what we were told by our government, a story then dutifully repeated *ad nauseam* on television, radio and in the press. So, like the vast majority of my fellow citizens, I remained blissfully ignorant of what the agreement was all about.

Several years later I actually read the text and became one of those very rare birds who had taken time off to do that. The scales fell from my eyes. The FTA was not really about trade, except in a peripheral way. The text made it very clear that the primary purpose of the FTA was to facilitate U.S. investment in Canada. The Americans wanted access to our industries and resources --especially our oil and natural gas and, soon, our water.

In retrospect this is very clear as Maude Barlow reminded us in an article in the *Globe and Mail*, "A 1985 U.S. congressional report called Canada's regulatory control over its natural gas a 'direct restriction of American rights to Canadian gas,' and called for the American government to make guaranteed access to Canadian supplies a point of national security. Ann Hughes, the ranking U.S. Commerce Department negotiator, was forthright about her country's wasteful energy habits, and admitted that Canada's energy, secured by the free-trade deal, would forestall conservation practices in the United States. Edward Ney, then U.S. ambassador to Canada, said later that Canada's energy reserves were the prime motivation for the United States in the negotiations."[5]

It is true that the FTA eliminated tariffs between the two countries over a ten-year period, but this was not a big deal because they were already coming off under the General Agreement on Tariffs and Trade (GATT). So by 1988, when the FTA came into effect, most items were already duty free and for the others, where tariffs still applied, Canada had an advantage because our tariffs were higher than those in the U.S. – an advantage that we gave up.

From the outset the two countries had very different objectives. These were stated during an initial meeting of Prime Minister Brian Mulroney's Chief of Staff, Derek Burney, and Senior Deputy U.S. Trade Representative, Michael B. Smith, on July 31, 1985.

Canadians wanted just two things. "Exemption from the application of U.S. Dumping and Anti-Subsidy laws, and a gradual phase-in, indeed a back-end loading, of tariff eliminations." The U.S. had two demands: "Immediate abolition of the infamous Foreign Investment Review Board (FIRB) and a faster implementation of Canadian tariff reductions, given the fact that Canadian tariffs were already higher than U.S. tariffs."[6]

In the end the Americans achieved both of their demands and Canada wimped out on both of its bottom-line objectives. We had to yield to American demands for accelerated reduction of our tariffs and, most important of all, we did not get an exemption from U.S. anti-dumping and countervailing duty laws which can be applied almost capriciously whenever the American political situation demands.

Consequently, we did not get the "guaranteed access" to U.S. markets that Mr. Mulroney so proudly proclaimed as a major victory. Presumably the prime motivation for the FTA from our side was "to settle the soft-wood lumber dispute once and for all." We blew that one because we couldn't convince the Americans to agree on a definition of what constitutes a subsidy. They preferred to set their own rules to suit their own circumstances. As everyone now knows, with just three fast balls across the centre of the plate Canada struck out completely.

They preferred to set their own rules to suit their own circumstances. So instead of hitting a home run, as the government and press led us to believe, Canada struck out completely.

While the soft-wood lumber dispute has been the most visible and blatant example of U.S. trade harassment, it is far from unique. Just ask Prince Edward Island potato growers, or our cement manufacturers or steel producers. More recently the U.S. has applied a tariff on durum and hard red spring wheat, saying both are unfairly subsidized. Wilfred (Butch) Harder, a Manitoba farmer and Wheat Board Director, said: "I just don't like the principle of the thing. Americans always talk about us subsidizing our producers, and we know very well that the ratio they subsidize their producers compared to ours is much, much higher."[7]

If there is one thing that knowledgeable negotiators should have known about the U.S., if they had done their homework, it is that "free trade" is an impossible dream. Fair trade, maybe, though highly unlikely. Free trade, never! The U.S. wants guaranteed access to other countries' markets but will never give up its right to harass competitors when politics demands.

So our team sold Canada down the river. We agreed to give U.S. investors "national treatment" status. That means that they have the same rights in Canada as Canadian citizens. This clause, which 98 percent of Canadians have never heard of, because they haven't read the treaties, has been the licence which allowed Americans to buy up more of Canada – much of it for as little as 65 cents on the dollar.

CANADA FOR SALE

The ink on the FTA was barely dry when Brian Mulroney flew triumphantly to New York to tell U.S. businessmen that Canada was "open for business" again. What he should have said was, "Canada is up for sale," and we have just signed a treaty guaranteeing that you can come up and help yourselves to our industries and resources.

From June 30, 1985 to June 30, 2001, almost 13,000 Canadian companies were sold to foreigners – the vast majority to our cousins south of the border. This figure only includes transactions subject to the Investment Canada Act. Furthermore, the dollar value of companies sold in 1999 was double that of 1998, which was itself a record. "You've got to be concerned that you're losing control of your own destiny," said Ian Macdonell, a partner at Crosbie & Company Inc., a Toronto investment banking firm which tracks mergers and acquisitions.[8]

A few of the better known companies sold include Aikenhead Hardware, acquired by Home Depot; Canstar, with its world famous Bauer line of sports equipment, by Nike; Club Monaco Inc., by Polo Ralph Lauren Inc.; Le Groupe Forex by Louisiana Pacific; MacMillan Bloedel, the icon of British Columbia's forest industry, by Weyerhaeuser; Midland Walwyn, Canada's last remaining large independent broker, by New York-based Merrill Lynch; the Montreal Canadiens hockey team by George N. Gillette, Jr.; Seagrams by Vivendi; Shoppers Drug Mart by New York-based Kohlberg Kravis & Roberts Co.; St. Laurent Paperboard Inc. by Smurfit-Stone Container Corp., North America's biggest packaging group; Tim Hortons by Wendy's; Trentway Wager bus to Coach USA. Some fairly recent sales in the energy field include Anderson Exploration by Devon Energy Corporation of Oklahoma City; Westcoast Energy was bought by Duke Energy of Charlotte, North Carolina; Gulf Canada Resources Ltd. was acquired by Houston-based Conoco. These three constitute the largest corporate takeovers in Canadian oil and gas history. They will not be the last. Even the largest Canadian corporations are not immune.

The sale of such a large share of the "oil patch" gave even former Alberta premier, and one of the strongest advocates of the FTA, Peter Lougheed, cause to reflect. In the course of a TV interview with Pamela Wallin, former broadcaster and currently Canada's Consul General in New York, he mused, on air, that Canada might have to reinstate the Foreign Investment Review Board, the agency Brian Mulroney dismantled as a pre-condition for the FTA. Lougheed would know, of course, that bringing FIRA back from the dead is not possible unless we abrogate NAFTA.

Meanwhile, as one enterprising retailer put it, "The Sale Continues." We are losing several companies every day, on average, and there is no end in sight. Not only that, but a number of those companies that have been on the "prohibited" list may soon be put on the auction block. Deputy Prime Minister John Manley warned us of that possibility as far back as March 2000, when he was Minister of Trade. In an interview with the *National Post* he predicted the end of federal restrictions that limit foreign ownership on Canadian airlines, communication companies and even banks. "It is coming down the road," he said, in what I considered a stunning admission from a Liberal cabinet minister.[9]

Slowly but surely Manley's prophecy is being fulfilled.
A House of Commons committee has recommended "open
season" for telecommunication companies.   And as Air
Canada struggles to stay afloat one of New York's biggest
vulture funds, Cerberus Capital, has begun buying the
airline's debt in a possible bid for control.[10]   This open
challenge to Canadian ownership laws will provide an
interesting test of the federal government's resolve.

In any event the trend provides a very black cloud over
Canada's future, and should give concerned citizens
immediate pause concerning what nationhood is all about.

Apologists for the sell-out of Canada's most important
assets tell us not to worry.   Canadians have been investing
just as heavily in the U.S. in recent years as Americans have
been in Canada.   Once again the figures are true but grossly
misleading.   For one thing the statistics don't tell us how
much of that investment was made by foreign-owned or
foreign-controlled Canadian companies.   Nor do they show
that a huge slice of the total represents Canadian banks'
expansion south of the border.   When one or more are
ultimately bought by American banks, and the whole bundle
goes south, the figures will take a dramatic turn for the
worse.

Ten times more important for the future of Canada is who
controls what.   Foreigners dominate many Canadian
industries including automobiles and trucks, chemicals and
chemical products, computers, electrical equipment, food
processing and packaging, glass, tobacco products and
cigarettes and heavy machinery.   Canada's total
manufacturing sector is now more than 50% foreign
controlled which is probably the reason job creation has been
slower than one might expect.

Now look at the other side of the coin.   As Mel Hurtig
points out in his latest excellent book, *The Vanishing
Country*, "There is not one single industry in the United
States, not one, that is majority-foreign-owned and/or
foreign-controlled, by anyone, let alone Canadians.   Only two
of scores of U.S. industries are remotely close, chemicals and
book publishing which are about one-third foreign."[11]

IF THE FTA WAS BAD, NAFTA IS WORSE!

It is important to know the origin of NAFTA in order to put its significance in perspective. It was President Bill Clinton's gift to the U.S. Round Table on Business in appreciation of its members raising the money for his re-election campaign. The tycoons wanted unrestricted access to an unlimited supply of cheap Mexican labour, so Clinton delivered. Canada climbed aboard so Canadian businessmen wouldn't be excluded.

The whole sad saga is recounted in *The Selling of "Free Trade": NAFTA, Washington and the Subversion of American Democracy*, by John MacArthur, publisher of *Harper's* magazine.[12]   Clinton deftly stick-handled the agreement through Congress in the face of stiff opposition from U.S. trade unions and liberal members of the Democratic Party. That Congress would allow the President to unilaterally change the U.S. constitution, and hand over to unelected NAFTA panels the right to make decisions that can't be over-turned by the U.S. Supreme Court, is a great tribute to his diplomatic skills.

Canada's automatic "me too" was a clear signal that neither the Mulroney nor the Chrétien governments were willing to uphold the constitutional rights of Canadian citizens. Canada, too, has handed over to NAFTA panels the right to trump our courts.

I am referring to NAFTA's Chapter 11, which gives U.S. and Mexican investors the right to sue Canada if any level of our government – federal, provincial or municipal – passes or amends any law that affects the profit, future profit or potential profit of that investor. The suits are settled by three person panels, meeting in secret, not subject to the rules of evidence and whose decisions over-ride Canadian law.

The problem about discussing this worrisome aspect of NAFTA is that just as 98 percent of Canadians are unfamiliar with the "national treatment" clause, almost the same proportion are unaware of Chapter 11. Often people think you are talking about the U.S. bankruptcy law, which sounds the same but which is very, very different.

The principle of NAFTA Chapter 11 is wrong. It gives foreign corporations greater rights in Canada than Canadian companies enjoy; and that is wrong!   Chapter 11 gives transnational corporations the status of nation states, and that is wrong.   A few Canadians are aware of the first suit launched against Canada under this provision, but it is worth repeating here because more Canadians should be aware of it, and reflect on the consequences for Canada and democracy.

THE ETHYL CASE

In 1996 the Parliament of Canada passed a law prohibiting the importation into Canada, or the distribution within Canada, of methylcyclopentadienyl manganese tricarbonyl (MMT) a manganese based gasoline additive. The reason given was that it posed a hazard to human health. The Ethyl Corporation, of Richmond, VA, filed a $250 million (US) suit against the Government of Canada.

When the Government received legal advice to the effect that it might lose the case it caved in to corporate pressure and settled out of court for $13 million (US), ($19-20 million Cdn.). But that was only the beginning. Parliament had to repeal the law under the terms of the settlement. So you have to ask yourself, what kind of democracy do we have when a private U.S. company can tell the Parliament of Canada what laws it can pass and what laws it cannot pass?

Equally obnoxious, the terms of the settlement required two cabinet ministers to stand in their places and read statements to the effect that MMT was not harmful either to the environment or to health. And this at the precise moment when the latest scientific evidence indicated that it was indeed harmful to the health, especially of children. So what kind of a world is it when private corporations can require cabinet ministers to lie to citizens about the hazards of commercial products?

Another U.S. corporation, S.D. Myers Inc. of Tallmadge, Ohio, launched a suit against Canada claiming compensation for a 15-month ban on the export of polychlorinated biphenyls (PCBs) dating back to 1995. The award was $5 million plus interest and damages. United

Parcel Service (UPS) is suing because it claims Canada Post unfairly subsidizes its Purolator courier services.

While there are other suits pending, or of which notice of intent has been received, the largest, by far, is Sunbelt Water, Inc. v. Government of Canada. The claim is for $1.5 billion to $10.5 billion (US) because the government of British Columbia changed the rules and wouldn't let the company sell our water.

This is the defining point. NAFTA Chapter 11 gives corporations unprecedented rights but doesn't provide governments or citizens with any off-setting rights. Elected officials, at all levels, can't change the rules in any way, even if it is clearly in the interests of their electors, without looking over their shoulders to see if they are likely to be sued.

ON BALANCE NAFTA IS A DISASTER

The Environment

For some people, NAFTA has been a success. This is no big surprise because it was designed to bring extraordinary government protection to a specific set of interests – Canadian, American and Mexican investors looking for cheaper labour and production costs. These are the same elite groups now pushing for NAFTA-II, an increased level of economic integration in North America but especially between Canada and the United States.

For the great majority, however, NAFTA has been an unmitigated disaster. We have witnessed a degradation of our environment, a considerable loss of control over our own destiny, the loss of many jobs, a lower standard of living compared to our American cousins and, finally, the prospect of Canada ultimately being annexed by the U.S. It is not a happy scenario and all the more so in the face of a new propaganda offensive which might be characterized as "if the medicine has made you sick, a bigger dose should help." Skeptics wonder if it's a case of cure or kill.

One of the downsides to NAFTA has been the impact on the environment. From the necessity of Ontario being forced to accept thousands of tons of toxic waste from the U.S., and risk further contamination of our precious water supply, to a steady convoy of trucks saturating highway 401 with Toronto's garbage enroute to its final resting place in Michigan, "free trade" has a high price tag attached. Charles Caccia, former Federal Minister of the Environment puts it bluntly: "NAFTA has been an environmental disaster."

An oversight agency set up under NAFTA is also concerned. Pulling no punches, a report by the North American Commission for Environmental Co-operation says, "The health of an environment that sustains 394 million people and an economy worth $9 trillion (US) is at risk."[13] As the *Toronto Star* pointed out in an editorial, "The fact that a body set up under the auspices of a free trade pact would point to the dangers of overestimating the gains from trade highlights the seriousness of the problem."[14]

The *Star* added that there are costs associated with economic growth and these are not taken into account in GDP increases. "By ignoring such costs, we could be vastly overstating our material progress. Mexico, for example, has calculated that from 1985 to 1992, the country's average growth rate of 2.2 percent is almost cut in half when the depletion of natural resources is taken into account."[15] Canada should take note.

LOSS OF CONTROL

The loss of control of our own destiny applies across a wide front but nowhere more so than in the field of energy. A prime motive, if not the prime motive, for Washington to promote the FTA was to gain guaranteed access to our fairly ample and easy to reach energy resources - oil, gas, electricity. This they achieved, and NAFTA now prevents us from selling our energy resources in Canada at lower rates than we sell it in the U.S.

"It also prevents us," as Linda McQuaig pointed out in one of her columns, "from cutting back on the amount of energy we sell to the Americans, in order to keep a larger share for ourselves - two things a sovereign country might want to do in a world where energy is one of the keys to a strong economy. (Mexico, the third NAFTA partner, balked at giving away such control and opted to stay out of the energy portions of NAFTA.)"[16]

It was really stupid of us to agree. Free trade is about maximizing "natural advantage." One of Canada's most valuable natural advantages has been cheap abundant energy. We have used this to attract giant aluminum reduction mills, for example. But when we make our natural advantage available to the Americans, as we propose to do with Nova Scotia natural gas, for example, New Brunswick mills can go begging as the gas and the jobs flow south. Little wonder that "New Brunswick Premier Bernard Lord has become the latest champion of the anti-globalization movement in Canada."[17]

The Americans are never satisfied, of course, so one of the objects of NAFTA-II is an even more closely integrated North American energy market in order to guarantee greater U.S. energy security. "Ironically, then, the thing the U.S. is fixated on – national energy security – is the very thing we have given up, under pressure from Washington."[18]

JOB CREATION

Proponents of "free trade" said that it would create jobs in Canada. If one can believe Brian Mulroney, that promise has been fulfilled. In a swing through the federal riding of Pictou-Antigonish-Guysborough on May 28, 2003, he said: "Free trade seems to have been a big winner for Canada. Four out of five jobs created since 1993 have come about directly as a result of free trade."[19]

If our former Prime Minister had been more forthright he would have added that for every three jobs created in the eight years after the FTA was signed four jobs were lost. The explanation comes from the Government itself, in the form of a little-known study commissioned by Industry Canada.

The authors, Dungan and Murphy, found that, while business sector exports grew quickly, import growth also kept pace. At the same time, the import content per unit of exports also grew markedly, while the domestic content per unit of exports fell. This means that employment (direct and indirect) in export industries rose from 19.6% of total business sector employment in 1989, to 28.3% in 1997. The rapid rise in imports, however, displaced (or destroyed) even more employment. The job-displacing effect of imports rose steadily from an equivalent of 21.1% of total business employment in 1989, to 32.7% in 1997. The authors conclude: "Imports are displacing 'relatively' more jobs than exports are adding."[20]

What did this mean in terms of actual jobs created and destroyed? Bruce Campbell of the Canadian Centre for Policy Alternatives derived these numbers from Dungan and Murphy's data. The result is striking. Between 1989 and 1997, about 870,000 export jobs were created, but during the same period 1,147,100 jobs were destroyed by imports. Thus, Canada's trade boom resulted in a net destruction of 276,000 jobs.[21]

THE INCOME GAP VERSUS THE U.S. HASN'T CLOSED

Another promise from the proponents of the FTA and NAFTA is that Canadian incomes would rise as a percentage of those of our American cousins. It hasn't happened. In fact the average GDP per capita is just a little worse in 2002, at 85.97 percent of the U.S. level, than it was in 1987, the last full year before the free trade agreement came into effect when our average GDP per capita was 87.5 percent of the U.S. level.

Chart No. 4 tells the story. It is the same story that Chart No. 3, net farm income, shows. In spite of increased exports there have been no benefits for the average Canadian. In fact most of us are worse off – relatively. If the per capita GDP compared to the U.S. has remained flat, almost, and rich Canadians have increased their share of national income, then the average Joe Canadian is significantly worse off – relatively.

Chart No. 4
Canada's GDP as % of U.S. GDP

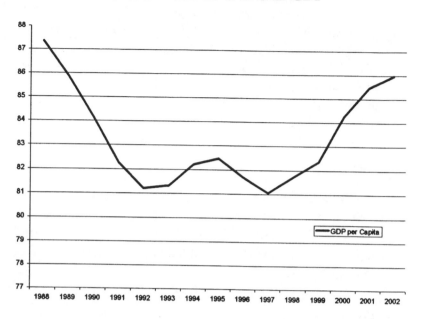

This is directly attributable to the FTA, NAFTA and globalization. It is my opinion that without the FTA and NAFTA, the average Canadian would be at least 5 percent better off today. So we have to be wary of people like Brian Mulroney, Tom D'Aquino, Wendy Dobson, Paul Celluci and the whole "free trade" gang as they urge even deeper economic and military integration with the U.S. They tricked us once with their multi-million dollar propaganda barrage, and they are gearing up to do it again. We were duped once! Will we be duped twice?

THE FTA/NAFTA SCORE CARD

	Plus	Minus
Some of Canada's richest people got even richer	✓	
Hundreds of [small] towns affected when U.S. closed branch plants		✓
Cost savings were not passed on to consumers		✓
The rate of family farm failures has increased sharply		✓
The distribution of income between rich and poor has worsened		✓
Foreign investors have greater rights than Canadians		✓
Canadian per capita GDP has fallen vs. U.S.		✓
We have given away the freedom to legislate in our own interests		✓
We have lost control of our energy resources		✓
NAFTA has been an environmental disaster		✓
Thousands of our best companies have been sold – more every day		✓
	1	10

Some score! Some fizzle!

As I pointed out in chapter 2, when Ronald Reagan signed the Canada-U.S. Free Trade Agreement he accomplished with one stroke of the pen what American generals and armies had been unable to do on several occasions – he conquered Canada. The conquest has been tentative for fifteen years but we are now approaching the point of no return. If NAFTA stays, and the FTAA is signed, it is game over for Canada.

NAFTA MUST GO!

CHAPTER 10

DEFENCE AND FOREIGN POLICY

"It takes twenty years of peace to make a man, it takes twenty seconds of war to destroy him."

King Baudouin of Belgium

A review of Canada's defence and foreign policy is long overdue. Should we support the trend toward U.S. unilateralism, and integrate our plans, forces and policies with theirs? Or should we reaffirm our support of multilateralism and pursue a role more independent of the U.S. even at the risk of annoying our powerful uncle to the south?

This chapter will not address all of the complex issues facing Canada in a volatile world. I believe, however, that we have reached a "defining moment" in our history and that the decisions we make in the new few months will determine our destiny as a sovereign state.

Before addressing the most critical choices we must make, however, I would like to take advantage of the opportunity to refute a widely held myth. I still hear people say that the present sad state of the Canadian Armed Forces is a direct result of the reforms I introduced when I was Minister of National Defence.

This is a monstrous untruth. To repeat it is really an insult to the intelligence of the naysayers because they are inferring that whatever I did was so perverse that for 36 years since I left the department it has been beyond the competence of 19 succeeding Liberal and Conservative ministers of defence to fix it. This is preposterous.

In fact the Armed Forces were in good shape when I and my immediate successor, Léo Cadieux, left them. They were reasonably well equipped – very well compared to today – and operationally ready. Their current state is the result of decisions taken after we left, and from years of neglect. To trace the decline it is necessary to turn the clock back to the days prior to the unification of the Armed Forces which were, in many ways, similar to those that exist today. Obviously something dramatic had to be done and unification appeared to be the most innovative and progressive answer.

THE UNIFICATION OF THE CANADIAN ARMED FORCES

Let me begin the story with the state of the Armed Forces when I was sworn in as Minister of National Defence in April, 1963, more than 40 years ago. Morale was very, very low for a number of reasons. The Diefenbaker government had accepted nuclear roles for the Royal Canadian Air Force (RCAF), both in Canada and Europe, and for the Canadian Army in Europe.

These included short-range Honest John ground-to-ground missiles for the army and bombs for the air division in Europe, air-to-air missiles for interceptor aircraft in Canada, and the infamous Bomarc anti-aircraft missile to be installed at North Bay, Ontario, and La Macaza, Québec. But having made these commitments under NATO and NORAD, and having spent millions to buy the hardware for the four systems, the government refused to accept the warheads to make them operational.

This upset the military who were the subject of some ridicule by our allies. One proposed solution, in particular, became a laughing stock. The Prime Minister suggested that the warheads for the Bomarcs be stored across the Niagara River in Buffalo, New York, and be brought to Canada when an emergency was declared. It was great sport to speculate how long it would take to get them out of storage, through customs, and on their merry way to North Bay while Soviet bombers were roaring through the skies.

The Liberal Party had been opposed to nuclear weapons. But when confronted with a *fait accompli*, and the very real possibility that Canada would be declared in default of its NATO commitments, Prime Minister Pearson reversed the policy and agreed that we should fulfill our obligations until new roles for the Canadian Forces could be negotiated. This decision was one of the reasons the Liberals won the election and I was given the mandate to implement the policy and review the state of the Armed Forces in general.

I found that morale in the Royal Canadian Navy (RCN) was near an all-time low. In September '63, *Maclean's* magazine carried an article by retired Commodore James Plomer entitled, "The Gold-Braid mind is killing our Navy." Plomer was merciless! He wrote: "In my opinion this childish obsession with the pomp of a bygone age is far stronger in the RCN than in any other modern navy."[1]

On the more general front, the previous government had established a Royal Commission under the chairmanship of Grant Glassco, to study the Armed Forces in depth and specifically to address the problem of duplication and triplication of effort between the services, with its widely-known and much deplored inevitable waste of taxpayers money.

Its principal recommendation was less than novel. In my opinion it was a cop-out. One of the commission's researchers said later that they had considered the unification of the three forces and felt that was the best solution. But they concluded it was not politically feasible.[2] So instead, they recommended that all doctors, dentists, lawyers, paymasters and other trades common to each service would be put under the command of the Chairman, Chiefs of Staff Committee. In effect, there would be four services instead of three, and the new one would even get its own uniform.

In my hands–on, close double-check of all this information I had some advantages compared to a number of novice ministers who had been put in charge of the department. I had been Parliamentary Assistant to Ralph Campney, when he was Minister of National Defence, and later his Associate Minister briefly before the St. Laurent government was defeated. I had spent a couple of fruitless years in the RCAF and then the Canadian Army and I had some significant experience in the aviation industry. All of this was a big help in separating the snow from the fog in official briefings.

The Prime Minister took me with him to London, England, on May 1, 1963 on his first official visit following the election. That gave me the opportunity to continue on to Germany and visit our Brigade Group which was part of the NATO force. I already knew that the tips of the Honest John rockets were filled with sand instead of warheads. But much more disconcerting was the fact that we had no modern mobile Howitzers; and our troops were equipped with ordinary trucks rather than armoured personal carriers for their mobility. I resolved to remedy these deficiencies at the earliest possible moment.

Later I embarked on a six-day visit with the Navy and the RCAF's Maritime Command. We flew first to Bermuda, changed planes, and continued on for a deck landing on the aircraft carrier *Bonaventure*. The next day I did a jack-stay transfer to the destroyer – escort *Restigouche*. The Navy missed its one big chance to drop me in the ocean. It was an exciting experience, especially when the sea was very rough, and the final instructions ringing in my ear as I crossed above the foam below were, "If anything goes wrong, let go." The "humour" was more obvious in retrospect.

The day was spent observing operation "Gouey Duck," an anti-submarine exercise. It was months later that I learned the log had been "cooked" to "impress the Minister." The official party flew back to Dartmouth in a big Argus sub-chaser at 350 feet off the deck (above the ocean) – a trip so rough it was just like driving a thousand miles on a washboard road – with the inevitable consequences for most of the party.

The final two days were spent in Halifax where I was directly exposed to "The Gold Braid Mentality" that Commodore Plomer had found to be so destructive. I soon concluded that the situation in the Navy was very much as he had portrayed it and this would have to be taken into account in any proposed reforms.

THE 1964 WHITE PAPER ON DEFENCE

Meanwhile, back at National Defence Headquarters (NDHQ) in Ottawa, I began to write, in longhand, the first draft of the White Paper on Defence, 1964. I had already concluded that the Chiefs of Staff Committee did not function the way it was supposed to. It did not set military priorities which would have been a legitimate *raison d'être*.

Worse, each chief – the Chief of the Naval Staff (CNS), the Chief of the General Staff (CGS) and the Chief of the Air Staff (CAS) – had direct access to the minister. So the first in line, with the best public relations, got his projects approved and the money allocated. The Air Force was usually the winner in this contest with its vastly superior PR. The Army, all too often, was at the end of the line and got little or nothing. It was a system where the "wish list" of one service took precedence over the needs of the Armed Forces as a whole.

Good decisions were always difficult, and often impossible, to achieve because each service put its own interests ahead of the common good. Attempts to reconcile differences were made by a committee system. In addition to the Chiefs of Staff Committee, there were 267 committees on every subject from the sublime to the ridiculous.

Committees were composed of five members, one each from the Navy, Army and Air Force, one from the Deputy Minister's Office (DMO), and one representing the Defence Research Board (DRB). They would meet for months before reaching a consensus. But the decisions were not binding on the Chiefs of Staff. So almost invariably, especially in respect of anything of significance, one or more of the chiefs would exercise his veto and the whole process would be for naught.

So my first major conclusion was that the Glassco solution was a non-starter. There was no point in having a sixth member of each committee when experience showed that it was a fruitless waste of time for five. The spirit of "non-cooperation" was so deeply entrenched that radical surgery was required.

My recommendation, which Parliament approved, was to lop off the heads of the three services and replace the Naval Board, the General Staff and the Air Staff with a single Defence Staff headed by a single Chief of Defence Staff (CDS).   At the same time the number of command headquarters was reduced from eleven to six. It was a lean, streamlined system which worked extraordinarily well and saved taxpayers millions of dollars.

The new organization eliminated most of the nonsense. There were no more end runs by a single service hoping to score with the minister. There were no vetoes of committee consensus decisions. There were no more cases of one service giving another the gears. When the RCAF had been preparing its submission to purchase the Argus aircraft for anti-submarine duty an air vice marshall had annotated a draft document, "This is our chance to screw the navy."

The new organization addressed and in most cases eliminated many old problems. For example, the RCN and the RCAF both used the Mark IV torpedo. But they had different parts numbers. Consequently, if one service was short of a part it was impossible to ask the other if it had a spare available to meet the emergency.

There had been a lot of duplication and triplication of equipment.   This   resulted   in   much   waste   and mismanagement.   There were many cases of one service selling surplus equipment at junk metal prices while another service was ordering the same equipment new. There was one classic case of one service selling surplus equipment to Levy Auto Parts in Toronto at scrap prices and another service buying it back at full retail price. In fact it was situations like this that had been responsible for the establishment of the Glassco Commission.

The new organization also muted much of the rigid thinking of senior staff, especially in the Navy. The old Naval Board had stoutly resisted the idea of bridge control which was being introduced in commercial ships.   It reluctantly agreed to lend a ship to the Defence Research

Board so it could install a mock-up bridge control for trials. Fifteen of the seventeen skippers involved in the test reported improved maneuverability, especially in docking.

The old Naval Board refused to consider the use of gas turbine engines in ships. They had always used steam – one wonders about the transition from sail – and that was good enough for them. They scoffed at the idea of putting "airplane" engines in ships and appeared totally unimpressed by the prospect of being able to perform a refit and turn-around in a matter of hours instead of weeks.

The integrated staff was much more open to new ideas and others' concerns. Its first meeting was historic. It was the first time in Canadian military history that senior officers of the Navy, Army and Air Force had sat down around a table together. Introductions were the first order of business. It didn't take long to get down to work and begin the design of a flexible, highly mobile force – organized on the basis of function.

The change was fairly well accepted by the majority of senior staff who knew full well that something had to be done because public opinion demanded it. So even if they were not wildly enthusiastic, their reservations were muted. They worked together on organization, plans and programs including the first five-year equipment purchase plan in the history of the Armed Forces.

Any controversies or major differences were reconciled at Defence Council. It was comprised of the Minister, the Associate Minister, the Deputy Minister, the CDS, and his senior staff in charge of the several functions. These included officers trained in each of the three elements. Council included a representative from External Affairs and one from Defence Production when equipment was on the agenda. The chief of public relations always attended so the press and public would be told both the decisions taken, and the reasons for them. It was a good system which produced good decisions.

STEP TWO – A SINGLE SERVICE

What had been accomplished to that point was generally known as "integration." And it might not have been necessary to proceed much further, for a while at least, had it not been for foot-dragging in the Personnel Department which was headed by a vice admiral. Instead of integrating personnel in those areas where it was intended, and sensible to do so, the old single service lists were maintained. This resulted in a plethora of complaints concerning different rules for leave, pay, retirement age and so on.

The urgency of the problem was driven home during a visit to Washington. At the end of a meeting with U.S. Secretary of Defense Robert McNamara, I decided to visit our Joint Staff Headquarters and talk to all ranks. When I had finished my spiel the questions began. They were all about personnel matters – the things that affect the troops as individuals.

Near the end of the session a corporal driver in the transportation section stood up. He told me that there were eight drivers in the section from three different services. Then the worst driver of the eight was promoted because he was the senior man on the army list. "If that is what you mean by integration," he said, looking me straight in the eye, "you can stuff it."

I knew at once that I would have to act quickly and firmly. The foot-draggers were going to continue their subversion in the hope that I would depart and the whole plan would be aborted. I was offered a change of portfolio but I opted to stay on because there was unfinished business and I felt, probably correctly, that if I didn't finish it, nobody would.

I was convinced of the need for a single service before the White Paper was written. The final straw was when I realized that the three services had each been planning for a different kind of war.

The Air Force was planning for a three to five day thermonuclear exchange; the Army was looking at a mobilization not too different from World Wars I and II; and the Navy for something in between. Obviously there had to be a unity of purpose at the top, supported by divisions appropriate to the strategy. So I thought of a legal structure something like General Motors with its component divisions.

It wasn't necessary to have a single service to adopt a common uniform, but I promised that it wouldn't be done without Parliamentary approval, so a new Bill was drafted to create a single "corporation" and, by inference, the adoption of a common uniform.

There were valid reasons for this. Having three separate uniforms for such a small force is not very efficient. This is especially true for some of the small, remote communication units with only a handful of people. Even the sunglass cases came in three different colours. The classic case arose when a female naval lab technician was posted to the Air Force hospital at Cold Lake, Alberta. Her pay and pantyhose had to be delivered by car, weekly, from the nearest naval reserve unit which was located in Calgary.

The colour of uniforms was a factor in representation and mind-set. Officers in three different coloured uniforms, driven in three different coloured cars attended local cocktail parties. But it was the habit of counting the number of personnel in the various coloured uniforms attending staff meetings to make sure that no one was over or under represented that got to me. This even happened when the subject being discussed was far more relevant to one service than another. The solution was to require everyone to attend in civvies so we could concentrate on the real business at hand.

When the Unification Bill was presented to Parliament it ran into ferocious opposition from the Conservative Party, quarterbacked by the recently retired Rear-Admiral Jeffrey Brock. The Admiral, incidentally, had not been fired for his opposition to unification, as widely assumed, but because he was the top man on the redundancy list. In any event, he possessed the leadership skills to rally the PC troops and the big and little guns fired from all directions.

Later, when the Bill was given second reading and was sent to committee, the opposition became even more intense.

Some retired officers spoke in favour of the Bill; others were bitterly opposed. I allowed serving officers to speak openly which was unprecedented under the British system. There were more ayes than nayes, but the nayes got all of the publicity. The press had a field day and public opinion, which had been highly favourable, began to turn.

So much so that Prime Minister Pearson got cold feet and was prepared to cut me adrift by letting the Bill die on the order paper when Parliament prorogued early for the summer, in anticipation of Expo '67. To say that I was disappointed would be the understatement of my life. But fortunately we had planned to travel together to Québec City to attend the funeral of the Governor General, George Vanier, in the PM's private railway car.

After dinner we had a chat in his room. I said that he was the boss and could do as he liked. But if he postponed the Bill until the next session he would have to get another minister to complete it. He said, "You're serious, aren't you?" "I am," I replied. He then said that the Unification Bill would be the only order of business before prorogation.

That was far from the end of it, and if you are really interested in how the political system works, and how nearly impossible it is to change anything of significance, you can find all the gory details in *Damn the Torpedoes*, my memoir of that era. But in the end the Bill became law, all of the debilitating uncertainty was removed, and we could get on with the job.

Meanwhile nearly the whole top echelon of officers accepted "golden handshakes" and were replaced by others who really believed in what they were doing. What a difference it made and what a joy it was to work with them. The unified Canadian Armed Forces had been born. And it had been accomplished without affecting operational readiness. On the contrary, it was enhanced by a vastly improved command structure.

A classified contingency plan was prepared at my request. It showed that with the assistance of one rented ship, we were capable of moving 1,500 troops to the Middle East, along with all their equipment in ten days - using our own transport. Contrast that with the present and you will see how much our operational capability has been degraded since that time.

For eight years, from 1964 to 1972, Canada had the best military organization in the world. The Swedes almost copied it, the Dutch were interested too. The Swedes sent a delegation to Ottawa with the intention of giving their plan the final stamp of approval. They ran into so much negative chatter that they changed their minds. Canadians, it seems, are genetically incapable of lauding their own achievements.

Would I have done anything differently if I had it all to do over again? Of course! Remember that we had no blueprint to follow. I wouldn't have fired Admiral Brock. Instead, I would have posted him to a NATO unit in Rome where he would have been as happy as a pearl in an oyster. I wouldn't have agreed to make all first-class privates into corporals, and I wouldn't have agreed to the green uniform.

In all three cases I acted on staff recommendations but there is no excuse, the buck stopped with me. I should have followed my own instincts, especially in the latter two cases, when I sensed that decisions were wrong and would get me into a lot of unnecessary trouble. One is much wiser with 20/20 hindsight. But the principle of a single armed force was right and I stand four square behind it.

THE TURNING POINT

Everything went quite smoothly until 1972 when Defence Minister Donald Macdonald, probably at the urging of the Prime Minister, decided to unify the civil and military headquarters and to make them into one. His initiative was implemented by his successor, Edgar Benson.[3] This, in my opinion, was a dreadful mistake You can't mix oil and water, which is exactly what they did with the hybrid headquarters. It was the beginning of the "civilianization" of the Armed Forces, and it has been downhill ever since.

Among other things, it was just the excuse the military needed to revert to their old ways. They began to establish *de facto* land, sea and air headquarters outside Ottawa resulting in four headquarters instead of two. The army re-established its pre-unification regional commands to prove that old soldiers never learn. The net result has been the recreation of a system not too different than the one in existence when I first arrived at NDHQ.

Inevitably this has resulted in an increase in the number of senior officers; a considerable amount of the triplication has come back; and the command structure is now more complex again, as we have seen reflected in one or two operations. Add to that the devastating deterioration resulting from 30 years of under-funding and you have to weep for the men and women who try valiantly to do Canada proud under excessively difficult circumstances.

And there are many people, unfamiliar with the history of the '60s and '70s, who hold me responsible for the decline. Even Maj. Gen. (ret.) Lewis MacKenzie, one of the generals for whom I have much respect, was unfamiliar with the sequence. In an article he wrote for the *Globe and Mail*, May 27, 1996, he said, "When then Prime Minister Pierre Trudeau and then Defence Minister Paul Hellyer ..."[4] He went on to blame the sad state of the forces on the amalgamation of the military and civil headquarters.

I phoned him at home and said, "General, I read your article in yesterday's *Globe* with interest and it contains much with which I agree. But I was never Defence Minister under Trudeau. In fact I had left that portfolio before he became Prime Minister." Without a second's hesitation, he replied: "Well I must say you are being very civil about it. If the shoe were on the other foot I would be (expletive deleted) mad!"

One distinguished detractor became better informed, but there are thousands more who are still misinformed, and that is the reason I decided to include this brief summary. For years I have said and written that the Canadian Armed Forces need two things to restore their lustre. First, to split the civil and military headquarters and recreate an organization more along the lines of the one I left. Second, they need an extra two or three billion dollars a year additional funding for the next ten years.

I wouldn't suggest that it were to be at the expense of health care or education. But it doesn't need to be. If we return to an economic system more along the lines of the one we had from 1939-1974 we can afford both. It breaks my heart to see our pilots and mechanics try to keep SeaKing helicopters and Hercules air transport planes, both of which were bought on my watch, flying safely. It is beyond all reason. Our soldiers, sailors and airmen deserve better. Much better!

ARMED FORCES FOR WHAT?

I used to smile when successive Canadian governments listed sovereignty as the first priority for Canadian Armed Forces. It was a rhetorical imperative. Once the niceties had been addressed, we could go on to the reality which was the necessity of cooperating with our friends and allies in the defence of freedom. In my lifetime we did that in World War II, in Korea, and as a contributing member of NATO and NORAD, dedicated to the containment of the Soviet Union with its particular brand of state capitalism called "communism."

So for more than half a century, since the United States entered World War II, we have worked in close collaboration with our friend and neighbour to the south. Our interests, if not exactly identical, were sufficiently similar that we were able to work harmoniously and effectively together. The one exception was the war in Vietnam. Canada wisely refused to participate in that misadventure, although we did provide discreet assistance in subtle ways.

With the disintegration of the Soviet Union, and the exposure of state capitalism as an inefficient economic system, however, the whole world geo-political landscape has changed dramatically. For the first time in generations Canada and the U.S. no longer have a common enemy. In fact there is no enemy of military significance posing a threat to North America.

The other side of that coin is the absence of any balance of power. The United States is the world's pre-eminent military power and is determined to keep it that way. In the absence of any real enemy, the Pentagon had to invent one to justify its grotesquely bloated plans, programs and expenditures. So it decreed that a handful of organized terrorists was sufficient to justify a "war against terrorism" that is global in nature and unending in timeline. It is essentially a cover story for world domination on behalf of U.S. commercial, financial and military interests.

It is a situation unlike anything Canada has ever faced. It is new. It is different. It is unprecedented. It presents Canada with an unhappy choice. Either we must aid and abet the Pentagon in its plan to run the world the U.S. way, even though that may be contrary to the world's best interests, or we must do the minimum, which is to protect the United States from genuine terrorist threats through its northern border, and otherwise sit on the sidelines to await the day, however distant, when the American Empire suffers the fate of all empires.

In "A Friendly Agreement in Advance," one of The Border Papers sponsored by the right-wing C.D. Howe Institute, the distinguished research professor of history emeritus of York University, J.L. Granatstein, concluded that Canada has no choice. His front page summary reads as follows.

"Canada has no choice but to cooperate with the United States on hemispheric defense and the war on terrorism. Hanging back would reduce Canada's leverage in negotiations with Washington and imperil its sovereignty if the United States acted to protect itself from attack without working with the Canadian government and armed forces. Canada must, therefore, make a serious political and budgetary commitment to strengthen the Canadian forces."[5]

That is a difficult paragraph to dissect. But dissect it I must, because I strongly agree with parts of it and equally strongly disagree with other parts. As I have already said, Canada must cooperate in hemispheric defence to the extent required to deter terrorists from attempting to attack the United States. And Canada must make a serious political and budgetary commitment to strengthen the Canadian forces in order to protect our own sovereignty. We have to eliminate any temptation the U.S. might have to patrol our borders for us.

It is Professor Granatstein's contention that we have no choice but to support the phony war on terrorism. I vehemently disagree with this. It would involve committing troops to American wars of "liberation" (conquest); helping to establish a global empire; and being an accessory to the Pentagon's diabolical plan to put weapons of mass destruction in space.

It is possible that the professor may not have read "Rebuilding America's Defenses"[6] before he wrote his paper, and that he was unaware of what the Pentagon is up to. If he was aware, I would have to conclude that his emotions might have affected his judgement. The aims of the "war against terrorism" are contrary to the world's best interests and totally inconsistent with Canadian values. And, yes, Canada does have a choice. We can say no! There may be a cost, but if there is we must pay it because our integrity and self-respect, as well as our sovereignty, are at stake. As an aside, I was bemused that Professor Granatstein would use the American spelling of "defense" on the cover of a Canadian paper. Most Canadians would spell it "defence."

A SPACE PRESERVATION TREATY

Canada's membership in North American Aerospace Defense (NORAD) was directly linked to the threat from the Soviet Union. That rationale no longer exists. So there is no valid reason to leave troops at Colorado Springs, which was NORAD headquarters, but which now is the home of U.S. Northern Command and the United States Airforce Space Command. Certainly it doesn't make sense to have Canadian Army and Navy officers stationed there as Defence Minister John McCallum recently agreed to do.

Either the Canadian Government is extraordinarily naïve or quite duplicitous. I prefer to think the former. They should know that there is no direct threat to the North American continent and that Northern Command is just another construct of the Pentagon's global pretensions. They should also know that any Canadian participation in what used to be called the National Missile Defense (NMD) is totally incompatible with Canada's longstanding opposition to the weaponization of space.

Just as the war on Iraq was justified on the basis of false information so, too, is the NMD. The alleged reason was to protect the continental U.S. from a couple of stray missiles from "rogue" states. The truth is far more sinister. Its real purpose is to give the U.S. a "first strike" capability against any power on earth without fear of retaliation.

The White House has now admitted that the shield will be worldwide in order to protect U.S. troops and their allies operating in any theatre anywhere. The Project for the New American Century spells out that it is planned to be a multi-layered global system to operate in conjunction with U.S. weapons of mass destruction to be installed in space. They will have the capacity to obliterate any civil or military target on earth and to zap any individual sitting in his or her back yard within a radius of a metre or less. That Canada may become an accessory to such a monstrous scheme sends shivers of disgust up and down my spine.

But Canada does have a choice! It can say "no," now, and pursue a positive alternative. It can convene a "Space Preservation Treaty Conference" as a matter of urgency, before it is too late. This is a marvelous opportunity for Canada to show the kind of leadership that the people of the world, including millions of Americans, are looking for. A treaty banning weapons in space could be followed with an international outer-space peace-keeping agency as proposed by Congressman Dennis Kucinich (D. Ohio). These are initiatives in the tradition of the brand of diplomacy practiced by former Foreign Affairs Minister Lloyd Axworthy with the Land Mines Treaty and the International World Court.

MULTILATERALISM

It is clear from the Project for a New American Century that the U.S. will only tolerate multilateralism to the extent that it is consistent with American commercial, financial and geo-political interests. When there is a conflict, unilateralism will reign. This is not the Canadian way. It is not in our best interests. Our adherence to multilateralism is a safer, better way.

No doubt we should maintain our membership in NATO, though with reservations. It was originally formed to fill a void created by the ineffectiveness of the United Nations to cope with the threat posed by an increasingly powerful Union of Soviet Socialist Republics. It was a defensive alliance which declared that an attack on one country would be regarded as an attack on all. It succeeded brilliantly, and maintained the peace for two generations until the Soviet Union collapsed.

As far back as 1964, however, the U.S. wanted to subvert its defensive nature and have it participate in the Vietnamese conflict. Wise heads prevailed, and it remained true to its principles. With its original *raison d'être* no longer in place, however, there will be great pressure from the U.S. for NATO support of its interventionist plans. Canada should resist unless the world interest is clearly paramount.

Normally, this would mean in cases where the operation has United Nations support, although one cannot rule out the possibility of rare exceptions in a system subject to veto power. On balance, however, the U.N. offers the best hope of consensus building and concerted action in the interests of a more just, peaceful and prosperous world. So Canada should continue to play an active and significant role in its deliberations.

We should also continue to support U.N. peace-keeping and peace-establishing operations. Our record is second to none in this respect, and the Canadian Armed Forces should build on their experience to help establish and maintain the peace in an increasingly volatile world. Their efforts should be backed up by a significantly expanded role in humanitarian aid and support.

Canada should also maintain its connections with the Commonwealth and with Francophonie. I well remember that when Pierre Trudeau became Prime Minister in 1968 he thought that the Commonwealth was outdated and redundant. Following his first meeting in London in January, 1969, however, he changed his mind. The value of maintaining long-standing relationships was compelling.

The case for maintaining ties with the Commonwealth applies to many aspects of our continuing adherence to the Francophonie. Our French ties go back to our earliest roots and this provides considerable opportunity for positive diplomacy in the interests of world peace and stability. It is an advantage not to be neglected.

In summary, Canada should follow its own Northern Star to the maximum extent possible. Canada's interests are not synonymous with U.S. interests, and we should do what is best for us, for the world and, in the end, for all mankind.

This is a policy that will not sit well with the present U.S. regime which has shown that it doesn't really care about us, even when we do its bidding. Consiquently there is little point in "going along" when we don't agree with U.S. policy and there is nothing to be gained. Even when we refused to support the war on Iraq, the wounds were only superficial and temporary. As Ambassador Paul Cellucci rightly said, the basic goodwill between our two peoples is too deep for the "disappointment" to last. The basic goodwill will survive regime change.

He was probably thinking that good relations will return to normal when the Chrétien government goes. I think of it as a two-way street, and that Canada's affection for Americans will survive the Bush Administration and revive gloriously when the great Republic elects a government that is as interested in the rest of the world, and its people, as it is in its own power and profit.

CHAPTER 11

A WORLD OF HOPE

"We must address the roots of violence. Only then will we transform the past century's legacy from a crushing burden into a cautionary lesson."

Nelson Mandela

I have already hinted that there is no hope of a just and prosperous world as long as the richest, most powerful country continues to squander so much of its wealth on killing machines. To be more specific, there is no hope as long as the neo-cons control the United States and attempt to impose their "values," under the label of "American values" by military means. The administration of George W. Bush constitutes the greatest threat to peace and security in the world today.

The concept of "regime change" is a two-edged sword. The current U.S. administration has already toppled two regimes and has plans for three or four more. Little wonder, then, that many thoughtful Americans are deeply distressed. It was serendipitous that ten minutes before I began to write this chapter an aide handed me a notice of Scott Ritter's new book entitled *Frontier Justice: Weapons of Mass Destruction and the Bushwhacking of America*.

Ritter, you may recall, is the former U.S. marine officer who served as a weapons inspector in Iraq from 1991 to 1998. In his book Ritter notes that the Bush administration's stated reason for launching the war was to rid Iraq of weapons of mass destruction. The book argues that there is no evidence that Iraq possesses, produces or concealed nuclear, chemical or biological weapons. Therefore, Ritter argues that "the United States carried out an illegal war of aggression." This former Bush supporter calls for "regime change in the United States at the next election."[1]

A damning indictment of the whole neo-con philosophy which dominates the Administration comes from Representative Ron Paul, a Republication congressman from Texas, of all unlikely places. In a July, 2003 address to the Congress entitled "Neo-conned," he addressed some of the most important philosophical issues of our time. The entire speech is recommended reading.[2]

In his remarkable address, Congressman Paul provides a list of 15 ideas that the neo-cons believe in. I will just include a few that I find most disturbing. "They agree with Trotsky on permanent revolution, violent as well as intellectual; they believe in pre-emptive war to achieve desired ends; they accept the notion that the ends justify the means – that hard-ball politics is a moral necessity; they are not bashful about an American empire; instead they strongly endorse it.

"The neo-cons believe that lying is necessary for the state to survive; they hold Leo Strauss in high esteem; they believe imperialism, if progressive in nature, is appropriate; using American might to force American ideals on others is acceptable. Force should not be limited to the defence of our country (the U.S.); they dislike and despise libertarians (therefore the same applies to all strict constitutionalists)."[3] [Leo Strauss was one of the most influential conservative thinkers of the twentieth century. He was a professor at the University of Chicago where he taught Deputy Defense Secretary Paul Wolfowitz.]

This is a philosophy so foreign to everything I have known and loved, that I find it totally repugnant. I do not believe in totalitarianism no matter how discreetly it is disguised. Consequently, I am appalled when I hear political leaders of various stripes, and business leaders of diverse organizations, suggest that Canada's greatest challenge is to re-establish cozy relations with the current U.S. Administration. It would be a Faustian contract. Instead, we should be polite, do business as usual to the extent that it is in our mutual interests and does not compromise our principles, and wait for the American people to do what is best for them, and for the rest of the world. That really means a total switch in philosophy from war-making to peace-making and prosperity-seeking.

ELIMINATE "THE ENFORCERS"

Not only must the U.S. undertake a massive shift in emphasis from military to civil pursuits, it must agree to the dismantling of those international institutions which have been the enforcers of neo-con values. I refer specifically to the International Monetary Fund and the World Bank. It is my opinion that both should be wound up completely.

In his book, *Globalization and Its Discontents*, former World Bank chief economist, Joseph Stiglitz, speaks harshly of the former. "The IMF's actions affect the lives and livelihoods of billions throughout the developing world; yet they have little say in its actions. The workers who are thrown out of jobs as a result of IMF programs have no seat at the table; while the bankers, who insist on getting repaid, are well represented through the finance ministers and central bank governors. The consequences for policy have been predictable: bailout packages which pay more attention to getting creditors repaid than to maintaining the economy at full employment."[4] That is really an understatement. Not only are jobs lost, but the poor countries are stripped of their assets at firesale prices.

Where Stiglitz and I part company is in the solution. He says there has to be a change in mindset on the part of the people running the show – the shareholders, of whom the U.S. is by far the largest. Not a chance! The mindset of everyone connected with the organization is so rigid that attempting to change it would be an exercise in futility. The institution cannot be redeemed, so it must be wound up and its assets used to help pay down Third World debt.

Stiglitz was, naturally, more charitable toward the World Bank, for which he was criticized. Michael Hudson, author of *Super Imperialism*, speaks for many critics in an interview with Standard Shaefer. "But Stiglitz remains defensive of the World Bank itself and continues to believe its goals despite no evidence that anything good has come from it, overlooking its complicity in promoting structural adjustments that have proved ecologically destructive and entirely in the American financial interests."[5] There was a time when I thought the Bank could be streamlined, reformed, made more transparent and more accountable – all of the clichés that I had read, or heard, emanating from world leaders and World Bank officials who realized that the institution was under legitimate attack.

The more I learned about the World Bank's operations and practices, however, the more jaundiced I became. In the end I concluded it had adopted the undemocratic policies of its sister financial institution, the IMF, and that there is no way it can be satisfactorily reformed.

THE WTO MUST GO

Based on its record to date, I am not a fan of the World Trade Organization. It is one more U.S. initiative that was sold under false pretenses. Allegedly its purpose was to develop a rules-based trading system. Its real purpose was to circumvent the power of nation states. So I am taking the liberty of repeating here some arguments and suggestions that I put forward in *Goodbye Canada*.

The concept of a rules-based system is great in theory. It sounds very reasonable. But surely not just one set of rules applying to all countries equally.

The World Boxing Federation has fifteen classes including flyweight, lightweight, middleweight and heavyweight. I would guess that the world's many different countries could be classified in as many as fifteen different categories. Certainly, not just one! The WTO rules were written by or on behalf of heavyweights for the benefit of heavyweights. The result is a trade regime under which everyone else is going to get clobbered.

The second objection is, as I said, the loss of democracy. The WTO exercises *de facto* executive, judicial and legislative powers equivalent to that of a world government.

These powers were transferred to it without the advice or consent of the peoples affected. Apologists for the WTO say that consent was granted when people elected the governments which did the deal. But that is a cop-out. The governments neither told their electors what was involved nor asked their opinion about it. Needless to say this was deliberate policy on the part of governments attempting to serve two masters.

The resulting loss of sovereignty is not acceptable. It is extremely offensive that the rights and prerogatives of nation states should be decided by unelected, unaccountable three-person panels. How does that square with the concept of democracy? It doesn't! It is all part of the plot to end popular democracy as we used to know it, and substitute a corporate plutocracy in its stead. Everything that men and women fought and died for is being taken away by stealth.

The only satisfactory remedy is to abolish the WTO and go back to the General Agreement on Tariffs and Trade (GATT) from which it sprang. From there we can build a trade regime which preserves the essential powers of nation states, recognizes the different needs of countries based on size, population and state of development, and provides the flexibility for cooperative rather than coercive relationships. For want of a better description I call them the "Marquess of Queensberry" Rules of Trade.

THE MARQUESS OF QUEENSBERRY RULES FOR TRADE AND INVESTMENT

- Fair trade, not "free trade." There is no such thing as genuine free trade, as Canada has found in its relationship with the U.S.
- Every country should have the right to protect some of its infant industries. If it doesn't, they will never grow to adulthood.
- Every country has the right to determine the conditions under which direct foreign investment is welcome.

- Every country has the right to impose controls on the movement of short-term capital in cases of emergency.
- Every country has the right to determine the limits of foreign ownership in each area of economic activity.
- Every nation state should have the right to decide what trade concessions it will put on the table in exchange for others as was the case under the GATT.
- Every country should have control over its own banking system including majority ownership.
- Every country has the right to use its own central bank to assist in the financing of essential services and to keep the economy operating at or near its potential at all times.
- Rich countries should be encouraged to license the use of their technology by poor countries at modest cost.
- Every country should be obligated to cooperate with other countries in the protection of the oceans, their species, the ozone layer and in all ways essential to protect the ecosystem for the benefit of future generations.
- Every country should be encouraged to maintain some control over its own food supply, to the extent practical, and not become dependent on patented seeds and products.
- Every country should have the right, and should be encouraged, to develop and maintain a significant degree of self-sufficiency in the production of goods and services for the use and enjoyment of its own people, and in order to reduce its vulnerability to the vagaries of decisions made by people far away who might be inclined to view foreigners more in the context of economic digits rather than as human beings.

Some may say that I am proposing a return to a "protectionist" world. Let me put it another way. I am proposing a system where the rights and interests of billions of people are protected from the predators – where the rich barons do not have unrestricted licence to poach on other people's estates.

The New World Order is a gigantic hoax. It has much more to do with investment and centralized ownership than it has with trade. The former has increased much more rapidly than the latter. In fact, globalization is a greed-driven monster which gains credibility from an economic theory based on academic abstractions far removed from the real world and real people.

Fundamentalist economics is a numbers game, in which people are digits. They are counted, sorted, exploited when useful, and abandoned when surplus. It would be numerically inefficient to treat them otherwise. The system I am proposing is one where human beings are entitled to a status greater than inanimate objects – one where they will have some control over their own lives and destiny. Such a system would be closer to the model of nature, where babies and children are protected until they reach maturity and can compete on their own. Even then, there are physical and intellectual differences between adults that must be taken into account.

What I am proposing is the transformation of a system which is immoral and inefficient, into one that is fundamentally moral and much more efficient – a system where everyone, everywhere, can hope for better things to come. To accomplish this will require some very major changes, including one or two new institutions to fill some of the functions now being performed by the old.

A NEW WORLD DOLLAR TO REPLACE THE EURO AND U.S. DOLLAR AS RESERVE CURRENCIES.

If I say that establishing a new world currency to replace the U.S. dollar and the Euro as reserve currencies is one of the most urgent problems facing the world today, many of you are likely to raise an eyebrow. The chances are ten to one that you haven't read or heard very much about it and that the subject is very low on your priority list of concerns.

This is not a case, however, of what you don't know won't hurt you. Quite the contrary!

For many years the U.S. has been getting a free ride with its huge balance of payments deficits. It has been buying a lot more from the world – much of it oil – than it has been selling. Normally that would result in a substantial devaluation of the U.S. dollar so exports would increase and imports become more expensive; or the U.S. would have to sell its assets as poor countries are required to do.

The U.S., however, has enjoyed a privilege not available to others. When it went off the gold standard, and refused to redeem U.S. dollars in gold, it obliged the world's central banks to finance its balance-of-payments deficit by using their surplus dollars to buy U.S. Treasury bonds, whose volume quickly exceeded America's ability or intention to pay. All of the dollars that wind up in the world's central banks have no place to go other than into the U.S. treasury. So the U.S. got the oil and other goods while the world wound up holding a lot of financial paper of questionable worth.

The U.S. "credit card" extravaganza might have gone on forever, or at least as far ahead as the eye can see, had it not been for the creation of the Euro. Despite its slow start it has become a fast-growing giant on the world financial scene, and has altered its geopolitics on a scale comparable to World War II or the collapse of the Soviet Empire. In offering governments and central banks a real choice of reserve currencies, the Euro has become a direct threat to the U.S. money monopoly.

As William Thomas points out in lifeboatnews.com, "Washington laughed when Saddam [Hussein] took the world's second biggest oil fields off the dollar standard and began demanding payment in Euros in October, 2000. The seemingly dimbulb dictator also converted his $10 billion UN reserve funds to Euros – just as that fledgling currency hit a historic low of 82 cents. The laughter stopped abruptly when the Euro's value crouched, then leaped 30%."[6]

Although the Pentagon planners running the U.S. had targeted Iraq as far back as 1992, Saddam's decision in 2000 increased the urgency of the project. "According to Aussie analyst Geoffrey Heard, the second brutal war against Iraq was intended to return Iraq's oil reserves to the dollar, intimidate other oil producers considering passing on the buck, and sabotage other potential Middle East players."[7]

Carleton University economics professor, and head of the Centre for Research on Globalization, Michel Chossudovsky, says that the war on Iraq was more than just the U.S. taking over the oil reserves, it was intended to cancel the contracts of rival Russian and European oil companies, "as well as exclude France, Russia and China" from a Middle-East-Central Asian region containing more than 70% of the world's reserves of oil and natural gas.

"No kidding" says William Thomas.   "A $40 billion Iraq-Russia contract to hunt oil in Iraq's western desert is now scrap paper. Ditto the rights of the French oil company TotalFinaElf to develop the huge Majnoon field, near the Iranian border, which may contain up to 30 billion barrels of greenhouse-goosing carbon."[8] Perhaps if President Bush had told the American people what was really at stake in Iraq, they might have been a bit more understanding of the French and Russian reluctance to assist.

Washington's greatest fear is that shift from the dollar to the Euro will spread. Iran and Saudi Arabia, between them, have the power to do incredible damage. Partly to retaliate against Bush's Axis of Evil rhetoric, Iran shifted most of its central bank reserves to Euros, and a move to use that currency as its oil standard appears to be in the cards. So far Saudi Arabia has remained faithful to the U.S. dollar but sniping from Washington has not gone unnoticed – a change could come.

What is going on now is a new "war" for financial dominance of the world. It is a "war" on many fronts – diplomatic, financial and military. The more any country dislikes or feels aggrieved by the U.S., the more likely it is to take the only action a non-military power can take against a superpower. It can switch sides in the financial "war" and win a moral victory.

The stakes are so high that the U.S. will do whatever it can to prop up its collapsing tent. The alternative, should

OPEC embrace the Euro for example, would be a massive devaluation of the U.S. dollar. So one shouldn't be too surprised to hear the neo-cons building a phony case for further regime changes in the Middle East.

Meanwhile, as always, it is the poor, the naïve and the helpless who suffer as a result of increased volatility in financial markets, greater uncertainty in economic forecasts, and further loss of life in unnecessary shooting wars – not to mention the need to pay for the conflict and then the interest on the money borrowed to finance it. It is a mug's game and all the world suffers. Needlessly!

The average person on the street may not really care too much whether it is the United States or Europe which gets the free ride – the open ended credit card. Or even if Japan should try something similar in the Pacific region. But it's not right. No country or region should be able to buy goods and services from their neighbours on endless credit. They should be required to balance their books just as their neighbours do. Short-term credit to meet emergency circumstances is quite acceptable. But indefinite, and virtually unlimited credit, with no intention of paying it back, is not.

A WORLD BANK AND A WORLD DOLLAR

The solution, which would put the U.S. dollar, the Euro, the yen and all other currencies on an equal footing, is a new world bank with a new world dollar. It could be called "The Universal," or "Uni," for short. It would be the currency of travellers' cheques and of central bank reserves. It would be, in effect, the universal world currency in which all international transactions were denominated.

The new world bank should be publicly-owned, by the people of the world, under a formula that would prevent undue influence from any country or region. Its assets would comprise very large deposits of all world currencies and gold. Each would be convertible into any other at market prices, as the bank would be the *de facto* bank of international settlements, replacing the highly secretive existing privately-owned Bank for International Settlements (BIS). It could also provide temporary credit to countries in need of short term help to fill any void left by the dissolution of the IMF.

The establishment of such a bank would be a major change to the world landscape. It would require a Herculean effort. But compare that to the alternative which will be continuous diplomatic, financial and shooting wars over possession of the endless supply of golden eggs.

THE ELIMINATION OF THIRD WORLD DEBT

I don't think there is much hope for billions of the world's poorest people unless they can get out from under the crushing burden of debt which makes them virtual slaves of the money lenders. In all too many cases poor countries pay most of their income from foreign sources just to pay the interest on their international debt.

And there is no light at the end of the tunnel. Just paying the interest on their debt is a bigger burden than most poor countries can bear. So there is nothing left over for principal repayments. In fact the principal owing continues to rise. Total external debt of low and middle income countries rose from $1.458 trillion in 1990 to $2.491 trillion in 2000.[9] So the only hope is debt forgiveness on a massive scale and the repeal of all conditions imposed by the IMF and World Bank.

Debt forgiveness by the rich countries, to date, has been picayune. Worse, there are often conditions attached. Poor countries are required to "reform" their economics, which really means adopt the Washington Consensus and open them up to rapacious exploitation by the big-hearted donors.

There are two very important reasons for paying off all Third World and most of the developing country debt. The first is that, to a very large extent, a substantial part of the debt qualifies as "odious." The World Bank, the IMF, private foreign banks and the U.S. Federal Reserve System have all been major contributors to what has become an impossible situation.

The World Bank and private international banks lent far too much money to poor countries, often for projects which did not generate enough income to repay principal and interest. Paul Volcker and the Federal Reserve made a bad situation impossible when interest rates were raised to intolerable 18% levels. The debt compounded. Then the IMF, and later the World Bank, exacerbated the situation by providing new loans so the poor countries could pay the interest on what they already owed, and the international banks could remain solvent. Sure, some of the Third World leaders borrowed the easy money with the fervour of kids in a candy store. But the lenders were equally, if not more culpable. So the wealthy Western world must be held responsible for a bad situation it could have prevented.

The second reason is enlightened self-interest. There is no doubt that paying off Third World debt is the moral thing to do. It is akin to admitting paternity and accepting financial responsibility for the consequences. But there is a bright side which cannot be ignored. Freed from the shackles of debt, the young economies will grow much faster and become stronger, more reliable trading partners in the years ahead.

What I am suggesting would be politically impossible if the $2.5 trillion had to be raised through taxes. Even the most warm-hearted citizens of the G7 might balk if they had to pay higher taxes for Third World debt relief at a time when their own essential services are being downgraded. Fortunately there is a much easier, painless way to accomplish the miracle.

All that is needed is for the governments of the rich countries to require all banks and deposit-taking institutions to increase their cash reserves by 1% a month; and for the governments themselves to create the money (cash) to make that possible. In less than two years enough money would be created to pay off the entire Third World and developing country debt. Individual rich countries' contributions would be proportional to their country's GDP, for the year 2003, in U.S. dollars as a percentage of the total GDP, in U.S. dollar equivalent, for the total list of contributor countries.

The United States would be the largest contributor at about $1.15 trillion; followed by Japan, at $440 billion; and Germany, at $220 billion. The U.K.'s contribution would be $170 billion; France's, $157 billion; and Italy's would be $130 billion. Canada's contribution would be about $80 billion. The Scandinavian countries, and some of the smaller European countries including Switzerland, as well as Australia and New Zealand, would also want to be included on the list as a matter of principle. The benefit to the world of operation "fresh start" is beyond calculation.

No doubt some of the bankers would claim that monetizing debt would be a tax on the banks. They would be kidding no one but themselves. Reducing their leverage would simply be restitution. And not full restitution by any means. It would only be partial restitution for long-standing gross injustice.

Banks have no inherent right to own assets equal to twenty or thirty times their capital, and collect interest on it all. This is usury gone wild. And while there is no way that banks can make amends for all the hardship they have created over the centuries, they can now, collectively, provide the world with the debt relief essential to absolve them of present and future crimes against humanity.

GOVERNMENT-CREATED MONEY

Not only is the monetization of some debt essential to renewed hope for much of the world, a better balance between debt money, created by private banks, and debt free money, created by governments, is necessary for the health, welfare and well-being of all human kind. Any system where private banks create 95% of the new money, on which interest has to be paid, is unsustainable.

An economy only grows when the money supply grows. And under our system that means that an economy only grows when someone is willing to borrow from the banks and take on more debt. But what happens when the debt level is so high that no one is willing to borrow more? First, the central bank lowers interest rates to encourage us to take on more debt. But when that finally fails to work, the economy stagnates due to lack of aggregate demand.

Look at some of the examples. The Japanese economy has been in the doldrums for years due to over-supply and inadequate demand. The U.S. economy began to slide before September 11, 2001 and is still hobbling along. The

Canadian economy has been operating well below capacity, and with high unemployment, for years. And now the German economy, too, is flat. And these are just examples, but some of the most important ones.

The world economy is in over-supply mode – which has been the plague of capitalism. Not that there aren't people in need of health care, education, food, housing, cars that pollute less, and all manner of things. But they don't have the money to buy them, and that is due to the banking system and the way new money is created. It is a big problem for which there is an easy solution. Governments must increase their share of the new money created, and the banks less. Not only would this end the threat of deflation, the world economy would grow at least one percent a year faster than it would otherwise.

Interest in this subject is increasing. Recently 26 MPs from three political parties introduced the following resolution into the U.K. parliament.

"That this House, concerned at the rising burden of private debt, public borrowing, student borrowing and public-private finance initiatives, notes that the proportion of publicly created money in circulation has fallen from 20 per cent of the money supply in 1964 to 3 per cent today; believes that increasing the proportion of publicly created money in issue could provide a new means of financing public investment; further notes' that the use of publicly created money can significantly reduce the cost of public investment by eliminating the need to pay interest; accepts that such a policy can be adopted without any impact on inflation if suitable regulatory changes are made; and therefore calls upon the Government and the Treasury Committee to commission and publish independent reviews on the procedures for and benefits of increasing the proportion of publicly created money in the economy."[10]

I wish that Canadian MPs were equally erudite. I hope that they soon will be because without banking reform our chances of building a strong, independent Canada are minimal. Later, I will be recommending that the money-creation function be split 50/50 between the government, through the Bank of Canada, and the private banks. I think that would be a good model for the world.

SEVEN GIANT STRIDES TO A WORLD OF <u>REAL</u> HOPE

1. The IMF must be dissolved and its function assigned to a New World Bank.
2. The International Bank for Reconstruction and Development (World Bank) must be dissolved.
3. The WTO must revert to a General Agreement on Tariffs and Trade.
4. "Marquess of Queensberry" Rules for Trade should be adopted.
5. A New World Bank and a New World Dollar should be created to end the "wars" for currency dominance.
6. All Third World and developing country debt should be paid off.
7. Private banks must share their monopoly to print money 50/50 with the people who own the patent.

CHAPTER 12

WHY PAUL MARTIN WON'T DO

"What is past is prologue."

William Shakespeare

This is a chapter that I truly wish was unnecessary. But my conscience will not allow me to take the easy way out. As someone who opted to put love of country ahead of both personal and party loyalties, I would be unfaithful to that choice if I were to evade the most important issue facing Canada in the next twelve months – the election expected in 2004.

My task is all the more difficult because I know and like Paul Martin, as I did his father before him. I sat beside Paul Martin Sr. in cabinet and in the House, and referred to him warmly as "cousin Paul." It was always my view that he would have made a much better prime minister than his detractors alleged.

Paul Martin Jr. is a different breed of man – quite unlike his father. He has been ensnared by the right-wing economic philosophy of Milton Friedman and his colleagues and the globalization agenda of the wealthy elite. This has already resulted in changing Canada's course from the pursuit of excellence to the path of mediocrity.

That, in itself, has been a disaster in countless ways, but it is now history. It is the future which is now of paramount concern. Contrary to the tradition of Prime Ministers Lester B. Pearson and Pierre E. Trudeau, Paul Martin is a continentalist who is firmly committed to deeper economic and military integration with the U.S. which is the slippery slope to ultimate annexation.

I think it is totally fitting that Martin should become prime minister for a few months as a cheerful vindication of the family name. Should he be given a majority mandate in a 2004 election, however, I think that would be bad for Canada. Consequently, I would like to present his record and his proposals in historical context.

In the 1993 election I supported the Liberal Party both financially and on the hustings. I was so totally disillusioned with Brian Mulroney and his administration that I thought anything would be an improvement. So I knocked on doors for Doug Peters, former chief economist for T-D Bank, who was running in Scarborough East. We were both ecstatic when he and the Liberal Party won.

I wrote the Prime Minister a letter of congratulations and wished him well.

"Now to the future. You have rekindled hope and expectations are high – perhaps unreasonably so. But I know you will want to fulfill and even exceed those expectations if at all possible. It can be done if the economy is expertly managed – which has not been the case for a long while.

"I didn't try for a nomination this time because your team made it clear that I was not welcome for "image" reasons. You know, "yesterday's man." But there is a way that I could help you achieve a miracle and that would be as deputy-minister of finance. Working as a team with Paul Martin, Doug Peters or John Manley would not only be a pleasure but I know that together we could produce spectacular results.

"I would not try to inflict my views on the party but I do covet the opportunity to sit across the table from the people responsible for making decisions and discuss options rationally. The opportunity had eluded me for a long time and to have it now would be a dream come true and a wonderful way to end my career in the service of my country – to try to keep it united."[1]

I also wrote to Paul Martin, who had been reluctant to accept the finance portfolio because he knew full well that no finance minister had ever become prime minister. I told him that his reluctance was well founded and that there was no orthodox escape from the mess that we were in. There was a positive way out, however.[2]

Needless to say I didn't get the call. Instead Martin opted for David Dodge, the incumbent Deputy-Minister of Finance, John Crow, the incumbent Governor of the Bank of Canada, and Peter Nicholson, a former banker hired for his personal staff, as his three closest advisers. It would have been impossible to assemble a more doctrinaire trio.

Instead of learning from history, and adopting progressive policies more in line with those in effect from 1939-1974, Martin bought the fundamentalism of the neo-cons. We were given the kind of policies which allowed Brian Mulroney to claim that the Chrétien government was a carbon copy of his own, and for the *Globe and Mail* to say that the Liberals were the best conservative government Canada had ever had.[3]

Doug Peters became so disillusioned with the advice that Martin was getting from his officials that he chose not to seek re-election. I was so totally devastated by the 1995 budget that I left the Liberal Party in the hope of opening up the economic debate to rational argument. The 1995 budget became the great divide between the Bay Street boys, who think that money is omnipotent, and the rest of us who believe it is only a means to an end. In fact, the 1995 budget was a disaster for Canada; and for anyone who understands monetary theory, which obviously Paul Martin does not, a totally unnecessary disaster!

In his epic war on the deficit, Martin slashed federal payments to the provinces by $6.2 billion a year, reducing federal transfers to $12.5 billion from $18.7 billion.[4] This massive downloading of financial responsibility from one level of government to another occurred at a time when costs were still rising.

CASUALTIES OF THE CUTBACKS

The first casualty was Canada's health care system. Despite the inevitable abuse, it had been Canada's social crown jewel. Its bedrock philosophy, that all citizens be treated equally, has set us apart from our American cousins. We lost our fear of the financial consequences of ill health. Now that confidence has been eroded due to cutbacks in service, longer queues for specialists and the slow but steady encroachment of a two-tier system.

Dozens of convenient hospitals were closed in the name of "improved efficiency," but an objective observer would conclude that the real reason was to save money. Hospital staff were sharply reduced; and in Ontario, at least, the last of its laboratory scientists was declared redundant because, according to one Ontario Ministry of Health spokesman, "It would be highly unlikely that we would find a new organism in Ontario."[5]

That was just before SARS, a new organism, turned out to be just a plane ride away. "The SARS virus made a mockery of government predictions and exposed the weaknesses of a stripped-down public-health system that many had warned was headed for crisis."[6] It would be unfair to saddle Paul Martin with specific decisions made by the various provincial governments, but beyond doubt the unravelling of the health care system Canada-wide began with his 1995 budget.

Other areas of concern in the health field involve the safety of our food and water. In his annual report of November 2001, Ontario Auditor-General Erik Peters said: "They [the government] have to do more to ensure the safety of our food supply."[7] He found there was insufficient testing of meat from slaughter-houses for bacteria, chemicals and other hazards. In addition, "Three or four of every 100 samples of fruit and vegetables tested by the Agriculture Ministry were awash in chemicals that exceeded allowable limits by as much as 80 times. Because of staff reductions, such tests are no longer conducted."[8]

Ontario is not the only province where under-staffing is a problem. Alberta's cattle industry generates $3.8 billion annually and represents 51% of its total farm income. You would expect it to have the best possible testing facilities that would preclude the necessity of outside help in emergencies like the Spring 2003 outbreak of bovine spongiform encephalopathy – BSE, or mad cow disease.

"Not so," says Deborah Yedlin, reporting for the *Globe and Mail*. "Instead, the pathology lab charged with testing is woefully understaffed, thanks to provincial cutbacks that saw the closing of five provincial health labs five years ago; and because of a mandate enacted last year, the testing of game is given priority over the testing of cattle. In round numbers that means the number of elk and deer tested last year was about five times that of cattle."[9]

Inadequate inspection not only affects the quality and safety of the food we eat, the water we drink has been equally compromised. The tragedy of Walkerton, Ontario, and subsequent revelations about the water quality in Ontario, and elsewhere, show us just how vulnerable and dependent on government we really are. Mr. Justice Dennis O'Connor, who headed the inquiry into the Walkerton contaminated water affair, said: "It is simply wrong to say, as the government argued at the inquiry, that Stan Koebel or the Walkerton PUC were solely responsible for the outbreak or that they were the only ones who could have prevented it."[10] In the words of the *Toronto Star*, "O'Connor also blasted the government for not ensuring that – after the privatization of water testing – laboratories alerted public health and environmental authorities directly of adverse results."[11]

Walkerton, though devastating and demoralizing, was only the tip of the iceberg. When the Ontario government subsequently changed the regulations to force more suppliers to test the water people drink, dangerous bacteria was discovered in 533 Ontario systems.[12] One would suspect that the evidence in Ontario is typical of other parts of the country.

MORE CASUALTIES

Apart from health care, few cutbacks have distressed me as much as those in education. It is a subject on which I feel most strongly. I was one of the thousands of veterans who had part or all of their post-secondary education paid at public expense. Universities bulged at the seams, but the federal government of the day gave us an opportunity that would not have been available otherwise.

So I am one who believes that post-secondary education should be universally available to all qualified students. But it isn't, as a result of reductions in federal funding of $2 to $3 billion dollars beginning with the fateful budget of 1995. Since then, tuition fees have soared. Now almost 80% of all full-time students need to borrow in order to attend college or university. Since 1990 their average debt load at graduation has tripled from $8,000 to $25,000.[13] This is no way to run a country.

The environment has been another area affected by the cutbacks. The Great Lakes clean-up was a typical and profoundly disturbing example. Millions of people drink the water from the lakes which also play critical roles in commerce and recreation. Setting back the time-table for clean-up and water quality improvements was a prime example of our warped priorities.

The arts have also taken it on the chin. For someone looking for a job, or struggling to make ends meet, they are not high on the wish list. But arts are the soul of a nation, its self-expression, and there is no area in which Canada has made greater progress since World War II. It has been a matter of great pride to see fanciful ideas survive the pangs of birth, the struggling adolescence and finally the adulthood of world class organizations.

We have come a long way, especially since the Canada Council was born. It has helped the larger more established companies and, at the same time, lent a helping hand to the smaller regional theatre companies, symphony orchestras, and talented individuals struggling to get a foot on the first rung of recognition.

When the cuts came, it became a struggle for survival. Some made it, some didn't. Even the major companies were hard-pressed to maintain their standards. The squeeze was short-sighted because not only have the arts flourished in Canada, they have become big business and an important tourist attraction, as well.

Not all Canadians love the CBC, but many who do love it with a passion. It has helped define who we are and what we are. It is part of the Canadian psyche and has contributed much to the interpretation of one part of the country to another. While most of us applauded the budgetary discipline that forced some belt-tightening, Martin's squeeze went much too far and forced the elimination of regional and other programming which cuts to the core of the system. One of my saddest experiences during a book promotion tour in October, 2001, was to walk past rows of locked doors and unoccupied offices in one CBC building after another.

DEFENCE

Nowhere have the effects of cutbacks and under-funding been more obvious than in the Canadian Armed Forces. It began, of course, with the cancellation of the EH-101 helicopter replacement project, one of the few positive steps begun by the unlamented Mulroney government. Ten years have elapsed and a replacement is not yet in sight. The situation is now desperate and dangerous for the pilots. As Daniel Leblanc reported in the *Globe and Mail*, "The Canadian Forces struggled earlier this year [2003] to find a replacement helicopter to accompany a warship to the Persian Gulf, after a Sea King crashed on HMCS *Iroquois'* deck."[14] Shame on us.

The situation with our 35-year old transport aircraft is equally bad. "Nine of Canada's 32 Hercules transport planes are waiting for repairs for small cracks in the centre wings, next to the aircraft's engines. Another four of the planes still need to be examined for the cracks, which are less than an inch long but can be dangerous."[15]

INFRASTRUCTURE

From coast-to-coast Canada's infrastructure is crumbling. There are roads, bridges, sewers and waterworks urgently in need of repair, upgrading or replacement. The list is endless but one example in the transportation field is illustrative of a wide-ranging problem of monumental proportions.

An editorial in the *Toronto Star* entitled "There's no cheap fix for Toronto gridlock," included the following. "Until last year, Queen's Park had cut off all transit funding, leaving cash-strapped Toronto-area municipalities to cope on their own. They couldn't. They were in no position to fill the void by funding the expensive expansions that were deemed so necessary.

"Now, we're living with the consequences of that failure to invest in public transit – the congested highways, crowded subway cars, the interminable waits for buses and streetcars and spiraling fares that make public transit less attractive... Despite Toronto's fast-growing population, the TTC operates 40 fewer streetcars, 200 fewer buses and carries 45 million fewer riders than just a few years ago."[16] These are quality of life issues.

CUTS CLOSE TO HOME

Few things upset my wife more than to read stories about the possibility of closing the pools in Toronto high schools. In her view, the opportunity to learn how to swim is essential for every young person. I agree, but it is just a symptom of the effects of under-funding. Music, drama, and other life-enriching subjects are being curbed. The same is true of physical education during school hours, and the public use of school facilities after hours.

"The Toronto District School Board has put a tag on the use of its sports fields and equipment as it attempts to recover about $1.7 million in yearly costs, but critics charge that it will limit access by community groups."[17]

"The Etobicoke Eagles football club paid $400 last summer to rent two fields at local high schools for use by its 250 young players. This year's bill for those fields: $12,000.

"To the north, volunteers who put together a summer mini-day camp for children in the low-income Weston Rd. area were once charged $53 to use a school playground once a week. The latest bill was $764.

"This is not just a Toronto problem. Maurice O'Neil, who runs a youth basketball team in Collingwood, has seen membership fees soar from as little as $50 per child to $400

after schools started charging up to $30 an hour to rent gyms.
As a doctor, O'Neil sees inactive children who have become
obese saddled with health problems ranging from diabetes to
hip and joint problems. He worries, as we all should, about
the long-term effects on kids' health by putting roadblocks in
their way to physical activity."[18]

FEDERAL / PROVINCIAL / MUNICIPAL / INDIVIDUAL / DOWNLOADING

You may say that many of the examples I have been
citing are provincial and municipal responsibilities. That is
true. But even though the neo-con policies of premiers like
Mike Harris, which favoured tax cuts for the rich to services
for the majority, were contributing factors, they were not the
source of our myriad problems. The source was Paul
Martin's 1995 federal budget.

Martin chose to balance the federal books by
downloading billions of dollars, previously available for
health and education, on the provinces. Hard-pressed
provinces had to readjust all of their spending priorities in
order to cope. So, many of them downloaded significant
additional responsibilities to the municipalities and school
boards, forcing them to play the same game by charging kids
more to play football.

The reason the former federal minister of finance has to
be held to account is because the government, of which he
was the key member, and the federal parliament which it
controlled, held the exclusive power over money and banking
which is the ultimate regulator of economic activity. Only
Ottawa could take positive action. It blew the opportunity.
Instead of learning from the experience of my generation, it
acted on the advice of the economic fundamentalists and
opted for the road to mediocrity.

THE ALTERNATIVE

The choice that Martin made not only caused irreparable
harm to Canada's social safety net, the cutbacks in spending
slowed the economy, increased unemployment and resulted in
lower tax revenues than would otherwise have been available.

In effect, financial problems were further exacerbated for lower levels of government.

The alternative was to achieve a balanced budget by opting for the full employment route. All that was required was to use the same creativity that allowed us to escape the Great Depression, help finance World War II and those good post-war years. A modest injection of government-created money would have employed more people, stimulated economic activity, and increased the GDP resulting in higher tax yields with which to balance the budget within a reasonable time.

In 1997 the Canadian Action Party retained the highly reputable Ottawa-based Informetrica Ltd. to do some computer simulations of what might be possible by means of a judicious injection of government-created money. The tests showed that it would have been possible to reduce unemployment from 9%, which it was then, to 4%, to balance the budget and to eliminate the hated Goods and Services Tax (GST), without replacing it with another tax, all within four years.

These results were so spectacular that Informetrica agreed to a joint press conference to release them. We found to our dismay that the press was not interested. It, like the officials running the country, appeared to be subject to an intellectual iron curtain that blocks out any real vision. There is far more intense interest in wallowing in the unhappy consequences of the problems than there is in honest attempts to resolve them.

WHAT IS PAST IS PROLOGUE

While it would be difficult to ever forgive Paul Martin for the inestimable damage he has done to this beautiful country, it would help a lot if one were convinced that he had learned from his experience and would lead Canada out of the wilderness to new heights of happiness and prosperity. Certainly he has mastered the rhetoric.

In a speech entitled "Globalization, Terrorism and the World Economy," that he made to a luncheon organized by the Reinventing Bretton Woods Committee, and the Conference Board of Canada, he included the following.

"Well, the time has come once again to follow their example – to let the greatest generation inspire us once more, to challenge conventional wisdom and inertia, to vanquish despair and to replace it with real and lasting hope."[19] Bravo! It is a paragraph worthy of the White House.

Unfortunately, the words don't match the music. There is a jarring discord between his call to challenge the conventional wisdom and his profound attachment to the status quo. Almost everything he believes and proposes can be found on the list of things I have enumerated as being detrimental to Canada's best interests. It includes all of the big ticket items.

Martin strongly supports the Free Trade Agreement and NAFTA, and would be willing to extend their scope and make us even more dependent on Washington. He backs the WTO and the Doha Round of Negotiations which will further limit our control over our own destiny. He would sign the FTAA and lock Canada into the "national treatment" clause which has been Canada's undoing.

The future Prime Minister is committed to both the IMF and the World Bank and would see their roles expanded. He is also a firm believer in globalization and the Washington Consensus. "More open markets must be a cornerstone of development," he said.[20]

The three, straight across the plate, strikes against Paul Martin are even more to be feared.

Strike one. "As he revs up his campaign to become prime minister, Paul Martin is promising to repair relations with the United States by increasing Canada's military and joining Washington's controversial missile-defense program."[21] That means he is willing to make Canada complicit in the installation of weapons of mass destruction in space – a concept alien to every Canadian value.

Strike two. "The big money has made no secret of its preference for Martin as the next Liberal boss."[22] He has collected $6.4 million in political donations ..."[23] This is unprecedented! It is absolutely impossible to raise that much money and not be indebted to the globalizers in the corporate community.

"Brian Guest, a spokesperson for Martin, dismisses the notion that the candidate's fundraising – which includes thousands of small donations as well as large ones – proves that he is the candidate of corporate Canada."[24] That sounds like the kind of spin that you would get from White House spokesman Ari Fleischer – and equally unbelievable.

Strike three. Letters he has signed prove that Paul Martin still doesn't understand monetary theory after ten years in the job where he was responsible for it. It is quite impossible to "vanquish despair and to replace it with real and lasting hope" until we have a prime minister who does understand.

CHAPTER 13

A REAL NORTHERN TIGER

"Nothing is more powerful than an idea whose time has come."

Victor Hugo

It is said that imitation is the greatest form of flattery. Whether true or not, I must admit that I was somewhat amused when Deputy Prime Minister John Manley borrowed a term I had been using for some time in a speech entitled "Canada: Northern Tiger, U.S. Colony or 51st U.S. State?" There were certain similarities in the portrayal of a better, stronger Canada. Further analysis is essential to determine the differences between the paper tiger and the real one.

In essence, I was saying that if Canada continues along the course set by the last two governments it will wind up as a paper tiger, or worse. But if we were to abrogate NAFTA, and replace it with a genuine fair trade agreement which would be in our own best interests, the way would be open for us to enjoy the best of all possible worlds. We could, in effect, have our cake and eat it too.

A precondition, of course, is the election of a better quality of government than we have seen for quite a long while. It has been so long that we have a whole generation of young voters who have never seen a good government and who probably believe that one is not possible. That attitude is understandable, but wrong, and could easily be dispelled by exposure to the real thing. By that I mean a government with a vision of how all of our assets and experience could be used creatively to achieve a new peak of excellence and opportunity for everyone.

It would have to be a populist government that would take power back from the Canadian "Permanent Government" – the Council of Chief Executive Officers, the big legal and public relations firms that work for the banks and large corporations, and the senior officials in government. They are the market fundamentalists responsible for the high unemployment, huge debt, chronic paucity of funds for worthy causes and the sale of thousands of our best companies to foreigners.

It was the Department of Trade, which negotiated the FTA and NAFTA, that put our assets on the auction block. It was the Competition Bureau, illogically a part of the Department of Trade, which refused to impose "reserve bids" in the Canadian interest. It was officials from the Department of Finance who engineered Paul Martin's disastrous 1995 budget. But it was the Bank of Canada which tops all government departments in damage done to date.

Ever since it adopted the ideas of Milton Friedman and his colleagues in 1974, it has ignored the mandate in its charter of fostering employment and economic growth, as well as maintaining the eternal value of our currency. It has concentrated exclusively on the control of inflation. Indeed, John Crow, when he was Governor, attempted to have Canada's constitution amended to make inflation control the Bank's only mandate. The Mulroney government, in the face of very strong opposition from all sides, declined.

The Bank operates as a law unto itself, however, and pretty well does as it pleases. The latest example was when Bank of Canada Governor David Dodge raised interest rates sharply to curb increased inflation which was due primarily to higher prices for energy and sky-rocketing insurance premiums. The former resulted from a hike in world prices and the latter to various causes that had nothing to do with the supply of money.

So, why apply tough medicine that will have absolutely no effect on the disease being treated? Especially when there are bad side effects like slowing down the growth of the economy at an inappropriate time, and pushing up the value of the Canadian dollar to make life difficult for Canadian manufacturers and exporters of resources.   We gained nothing and lost quite a bit from the Bank's misguided policy. Is that rational?

The problem with market fundamentalism is its lack of rationality. The Bank of Canada has proved that in spades several times, the most devastating being in 1981-82 when Bank of Canada Governor Gerald Bouey followed Federal Reserve Chairman Paul Volcker in raising interest rates to ridiculous highs – 18% in the U.S. and 22% in Canada – to induce the most devastating recession since the Great Depression of the 1930s.

Literally thousands of Canadians lost their homes when they couldn't afford the high interest rates; thousands of entrepreneurs went bankrupt when the economy slowed down; thousands of farmers lost their farms, in many cases after four or five generations in the family; and about half a million Canadian men and women lost their jobs. All of this as a result of one of the most hard-hearted and inhumane maneuvers in history. And it was all unnecessary. A simple incomes policy, designed to curb the excesses of monopoly and market power, would have reduced inflation further and faster – and without a single job being lost.

That wasn't tried, however, and unemployment rose to tragically high levels. The Trudeau government came under attack, and responded by creating new programs to provide jobs. Just stop to think about what was really happening. One branch of government, the Bank of Canada, deliberately and callously put half-a-million people out of work. Then other branches of that same government started scrambling around trying to dream up new programs designed to put a few of those same people back to work. Can you think of any greater insanity?

Naturally the politicians were blamed for repairing some of the damage caused by the Bank of Canada's tight money policy and the deficits and debt that flowed from it. But that really isn't fair. Of the $574 billion net public debt at the end of the fiscal year 1995/96, less than 5 percent was due to program spending. All the rest was due to compound interest which could have been largely if not entirely avoided if the Bank of Canada had been working for us rather than against us. Monetary policy was at total cross purposes with fiscal policy.

THE CHANGING OF THE GUARD

This lengthy preamble is meant to say that Canada can never be more than a paper tiger unless a new government grabs the reins of power and uses it intelligently. One of the first things I learned about economics is that monetary policy (the availability of money and the interest rate charged for it) and fiscal policy (the rate of increase or decrease in government expenditures) should work together in total harmony rather than tugging in opposite directions. If governments need to increase expenditures to provide jobs, and get the economy up to its best operating potential, then the Bank of Canada should make that possible. That is the reason it was created – to free us from the economic fundamentalism of the 1920s and 1930s.

What a Real Tiger Could Do

When you see a list of the things that politicians say need to be done you will probably agree with most – perhaps all of the items. But anyone who tells you that they will address the problems, without telling you where the money is coming from, is not levelling with you. So cynicism reigns. First, however, let's review a few of the urgent needs.

Health Care

The federal government has restored most of the money it cut back in 1995, yet the provincial governments' claim, and most independent observers agree, that at least another $3 billion a year is required to provide the kind of service that is needed and expected by long-suffering citizens.

Education

There is little point in a more highly educated workforce if the best jobs migrate with ownership of our industries. A real tiger will stop the sell-off, however, so the goal should be universal access to post-secondary education. Two billion dollars a year to reduce tuition fees would help toward achieving that goal. Another billion or so is needed to make sure swimming pools don't close, music and drama are restored, more money is available for special needs children, and that youngsters and other community groups can use playing fields and other school facilities after hours at prices they can afford.

The Environment

To achieve our Kyoto greenhouse gas reduction targets will cost a lot of money – the Chamber of Commerce estimate is $30 billion by 2010.[1] But that is not our only environmental concern. "Based on discussions with federal officials, the environmental group Mining Watch Canada estimates Ottawa's liability for abandoned mines to be about $640 million. But that could soar to an additional $1 billion when it includes the clean-up at the Giant Gold Mine near Yellowknife."[2] One of the last pristine fresh water lakes in the world is at stake. Then there is the decades overdue clean-up of the tar pond at Sydney, Nova Scotia, and the list goes on and on.

"Dismantling Ontario's nuclear power reactors and safely getting rid of radioactive waste will cost about $18 billion and take until 2070 according to official estimates" by the provincially owned Ontario Power Generation company.[3] Where will the money come from?

Affordable Housing

This is a project close to my heart. The extent of homelessness in Canada is a national disgrace, due in part to the budget cutbacks of the 1990s. Any civilized country should be able to afford a roof over the head of its citizens. Certainly a cold country like Canada should. It will take at least $1 billion a year to make the slightest dent in the backlog of almost half-a-million units.

Transportation

"Congestion and issues related to transportation are coming up now as one of the leading areas of concern for the business community, equal to, if not higher than, taxation," Elyse Allen said, during a panel called Making Transportation Work.[4] The situation is now so bad that it is not just the quality of life that has been affected, but the cost of doing business, as well. In Toronto alone, "There's an $800 million a year capital shortfall for roads and transit and another $500 million a year operating shortfall to fund transit growth."[5]

The sums required are so great that urban planner Joe Berridge says, "Tolls are coming. That's the only place the money is going to come from on the scale we need."[6]

That is the conventional solution, but it is not the only one and certainly not the best one. Highway 407 is a perfect example of private exploitation of a public necessity.

Rail and air transportation could also benefit from a major cash infusion. We have been told that the federal government is considering a plan to spend as much as $3 billion to upgrade the railway system.[7] At the same time millions are needed to reduce the myriad surcharges that are putting air travel within Canada out of range of many Canadians wishing to visit other parts of their own country.

Infrastructure

While the requirements for road, rail and air are quite obvious there are other pressing need for infrastructure upgrades – some of them underground. There are sewers and sewage disposal systems to be brought up to standard. Our waterworks are urgently in need of sophisticated new equipment to improve the quality of the water we drink and filter out more of the microorganisms which can pose a danger to human health. The state of any country's infrastructure is a signpost of excellence and ours is in need of a lot of improvement.

This section shouldn't end without mentioning the need for vast sums to finance the construction of new power generating facilities to meet both Kyoto targets and increased demand.

Farmers and Fishermen

After the extensive coverage that I gave to the farmers in an earlier chapter it would be inappropriate to omit their needs on the list of accounts. Whether it be drought, grasshoppers, competition from countries where farmers receive bigger subsidies, or borders closed to beef exports as a result of BSE, our farmers need help if they are to survive.

The same is true of fishermen due to species depletion, low quotas or no quotas. Canadians will have to supplement incomes by at least a billion dollars or so if we are to keep the source of our domestic food supply alive and solvent.

The Arts and the CBC

In the previous chapter I mentioned the slippage that has occurred as a result of cutbacks in funding. The time has come to play catch-up. And when that has been achieved, increase funding modestly but consistently in the pursuit of even higher levels of excellence.

And to those who would privatize the CBC, or cut its funding even further, let me remind you that almost every singer, actor, comedian and commentator who has made it "big time" in the U.S., and to whom we point with pride, got his or her start with mother corporation.

The Armed Forces

The needs of the Canadian Armed Forces are so well known that there is no need to recapitulate them here. If we want to remain a sovereign country, and play any significant role in maintaining the peace and security of the world, we have to ante up.

Despite the incredible handicaps under which they have been operating, man for man and woman for woman, the members of the Canadian Armed Forces are as good as any in the world, and better than most. But they are understaffed and badly equipped. They need an extra $2 to $3 billion a year to regain their pride, and ours in their operational capability.

WHERE WILL THE MONEY COME FROM?

It should be patently obvious to anyone who can count that even the partial list of needs enumerated above cannot be financed from tax revenues. The amount of money urgently required is five to ten times greater than will be available from that source.

The situation could become even more desperate. "Can Canada's surplus survive harder times?" the *Globe and Mail* asked in a lead editorial.[8] The answer is no. That is the way fundamentalist economics works. An economy peters out periodically. Then you have to have a new invention like railways, airplanes or computers, or a new war so that people, business or governments will start borrowing more to increase the money supply and revive the system.

That's what happened with World War II. The Government of Canada, through the Bank of Canada, printed a lot of money to help finance the war and the private banks printed the balance required. The system worked. Somehow, however, we seem incapable of applying the same intelligent solutions to win the peace as we did to win the war. What we need, then, is not another shooting war, but a war against ill-health, homelessness, poverty, etc.

If, instead of letting the private banks print 95% of the new money each year, the function were split 50/50 between them and the government, on behalf of the people who own the right, there would be enough money available to attack all the problems listed in this chapter at a reasonable and sustainable rate. The federal government would have about $15 billion a year in extra revenue to share with the provinces and municipalities.

The extra expenditures would reduce unemployment, increase the GDP and consequently the tax yields. There would be enough revenue in total to meet all legitimate demands with enough left over for modest tax cuts and debt reduction – perhaps at the rate of 1% a year. Monetary reform, then, can be the bridge between the left and the right in politics – the legitimate concerns of each can be addressed.

The mechanism I propose for government-created money (GCM) is a variation on that used in World War II. Instead of the Bank of Canada printing money to buy government bonds, it would buy federal government issued non-callable, non-transferable common shares in Canada, with par value of $1 billion each. This method has the advantage of being simpler and not adding to our already excessive debt. As for the principle involved, I agree with Thomas Edison, an inventive genius who understood monetary theory, who said, "If the nation can issue a dollar bond it can issue a dollar bill. The element that makes the bond good makes the bill good."

The concept of using GCM to mitigate stagnation and possible deflation is gaining greater currency. Not only are British MPs showing interest, "The *Economist* and other conservative voices are now calling on the Bank of Japan to 'print money' to get the Japanese economy out of its current deflationary spiral."[9] I agree, of course, because that is the same advice I put forward in *Goodbye Canada*. It is needed, though less desperately, in many countries including our own.

Any system involving a larger role for the government in money creation will require an amendment to the Bank Act reinstating cash reserve requirements for the banks and other deposit-taking institutions. At the rate I have proposed, they would have to increase cash reserves by about 1.8% a year, which is far from onerous, and which would have minimal, if any, effect on bank profits. Other measures would be required to ensure that foreign banks were denied any advantage as a result.

THE TWO OBJECTIONS ARE SPURIOUS

The first concern is that GCM would be inflationary. At a conference a few years ago, when unemployment was high and the economy in the doldrums, I suggested that we learn from earlier experience and use GCM to resolve an obvious problem. David Dodge, the then Deputy Minister of

Finance, said "Mr. Hellyer's solution would be inflationary," when he was designated to reply.

Not so! As anyone who has studied any economics knows, or should know, it is the quantity of money which is put into circulation that determines prices. Not who prints it. There may be times, as in the 2003 slowdown, when you want to increase the volume to stimulate an economy operating well below its potential. But that decision has no bearing on who creates the money.

The second objection is referred to as "crowding out." That means that money the government creates and spends is not available to private industry. This is true but requires analysis. Bank lending for industrial expansion has been a small part of the total. Far too much has been lent to buy stocks and bonds on margin, and for acquisitions and takeovers, including the banks' own purchases of foreign companies.

The Royal Bank lent Loblaws Chairman Galen Weston $1.4 billion to buy Selfridges in England.[10] That huge monetary expansion would not create one new job in Canada. It would not build one new house. If space permitted I could give other examples of money creation far removed from the spirit of the licences with which the banks have been endowed. The bottom line is that the banks would still have lots of leeway to finance real economic expansion. If the day arose when that were not so, the government could always provide a little extra leeway, temporarily, as required.

There is absolutely no way Canada can become a real Northern Tiger without the judicious use of government-created money. With it we can win the myriad wars against mediocrity and become a model for the world to emulate. There will be exciting opportunities for young Canadians and for others who choose to come here and share our bounty. We will have "one big party," metaphorically speaking.

CHAPTER 14

ONE BIG PARTY

"There is a tide in the affairs of men, which taken at the flood, leads on to fortune;omitted, all the voyage of their life is bound in shallows and in miseries."

William Shakespeare

Even many of my Liberal friends agree that it is time for a change of government in Ottawa. After three terms in office any party is inclined to become arrogant and somewhat corrupt. The Liberal Party is no exception. Add to this the certainty that Paul Martin, as prime minister, will lead us further into the arms of a U.S. Administration which is quite unrepresentative of the majority of the American people, and the need for change becomes urgent – in the extreme.

We are headed for ultimate annexation, which is part of the Bush administration's plan for empire, without being given the opportunity to determine the outcome. The die will be cast long before millions of Canadians become alive to what is really going on with the corporate elite in Canada and the world. It has always been my position that if the Canadian people voted to join the U.S., I wouldn't like it but I would accept the verdict because I am a democrat. To have it become a fait accompli without being given the right to choose, however, is not my brand of democracy.

Even though a change in government in Ottawa appears to be essential, if we want to save Canada and keep it independent, many of us – probably a majority – feel totally disenfranchised when we look at the alternatives available to us. Change we want! But change to what and to whom?

The Alliance is the nearest thing to a mirror image of the U.S. Republican Party that one would be likely to find anywhere. Its leader, Stephen Harper, is the leader of the "me too" brigade when it comes to marching in lock step with the White House. For Canadian patriots, voting for the Alliance would be like jumping out of the frying pan into the fire.

The Progressive Conservative Party would only be marginally less hopeless. Two of Peter MacKay's leadership opponents had him tagged accurately when they described him as the "status quo" candidate. His controversial deal with David Orchard should provide no solace for patriots. It was just game playing to get him over a big hurdle on the obstacle course to leadership.

In his first newsletter following the convention, and later repeated in a speech to the Confederation Club on June 19th, MacKay said, "Let me make myself completely clear on this point. I completely and unequivocally support NAFTA and the Canada-U.S. Free Trade Agreement. We created these agreements. It will remain our policy bedrock – the crown jewel." Nothing could be clearer than that. The PC Party remains the party of Brian Mulroney, Conrad Black, Peter White and the Bay Street boys.

My sad but certain conclusion is that neither the Alliance nor the PCs would change anything of significance in the critical areas of economics and trade. They would be strictly status quo. Writing this reminded me of my early days as a proud Liberal when it upset me greatly to hear Tommy Douglas or David Lewis say that it didn't matter whether the Liberals or Conservatives were elected. We were Tweedle-dum and Tweedle-dee. I was angry because I recognized the truth of what they were saying – differences between the two major parties were minor rather than substantial.

CANADA NEEDS A REAL CHOICE

At the time of writing the vast majority of Canadians just assume that the Liberal Party will be swept back into office at the next election. That conclusion is based on the certainty that none of the other four parties represented in the House of

Commons has a hope in Hades of successfully challenging the incumbent. Although Canadians would greatly prefer a two-party system, with a "government in waiting" in the wings, none of the alternatives is sufficiently appealing to voters to be given that mantle.

Consequently, for about three years now, I have been promoting the idea of a big, new, broadly-based, progressive pro-Canada party. It would be new in almost every sense of the word. It would not be controlled by either big business or labour, and would be free to represent all Canadians equally. It would be a party that would have the guts to abrogate NAFTA, promote fair trade and stop the firesale of Canadian assets and resources. It would be a party with the intelligence to use the Bank of Canada creatively to win the peace and transform an independent Canada into a real Northern Tiger.

At last Canadians would have the opportunity to elect a government that could stop the constant quibbling between federal, provincial and municipal levels of government which drives citizens to distraction. An agreement could be reached which would provide each level of government with revenues adequate to cope with its responsibilities. Wouldn't it be wonderful to see important projects get underway in weeks or months rather than years or decades?

May I make it abundantly clear that when I talk about a new party, I do not mean an additional party. We have too many parties already! Two or more of the existing parties should merge and be transformed into a dynamic new entity embodying principles along the lines described above. Canada needs something radically different, and better.

One might wish that two of the four opposition parties would agree to get together for this purpose. Realistically, however, it isn't going to happen; and certainly not in the few short months before a 2004 election. There is too much nostalgia for days of former glory, ego and turf protection involved.

Of the four, the New Democratic Party is the one which appears to be the most open to change. The new legislation prohibiting donations from unions will help facilitate a process which was already being talked about before the measure was introduced. Above all, the NDP has in Jack Layton the only leader with the potential for the critically important job at hand.

JACK LAYTON HAS POTENTIAL

I don't know Jack Layton as well as I knew his father who was a friend and supporter of mine for many years. But I have followed Jack's career in municipal politics for a long while, and I have seen him mature and mellow. He is a man of compassion who really cares about the poor and the homeless. At the same time he is well aware that you can't have a high quality of life in the cities unless you build the infrastructure and provide the services necessary for business and labour to generate the wealth essential to that end.

Another big plus is that he is the first leader of one of the major parties to understand monetary theory since Wm. Lyon Mackenzie King led the Liberal Party in the 1930s and '40s. As I suggested earlier, this is the great divide between the paper tigers and the real ones. It is not a left wing idea. It is really radicalism in the best dictionary sense of the word – essential and fundamental. May I remind you, too, that it is the bridge between left and right in politics.

Layton is left of centre on the old political scale. But much of the problem is rhetoric rather than reality. If you start ticking off the issues listed in the previous chapter the majority of Canadians will be 80% to 90% in agreement, and that is what counts. Layton is not as far left as Pierre Trudeau was when he became leader of the Liberal Party. Yet Trudeau was accepted by a solid majority of Canadians.

So I hope Jack will forgive me if I say that, in my opinion, he is the only genuine small "l" liberal who will be leading a major party in the next general election. His current hurdle lies in the fact that he is the leader of a party that can't win. For emotional and historical reasons more than 50% of Canadians will not even consider voting NDP.

Yet the NDP can play a critically important role in the reshuffling of the Canadian political deck. So on June 25, 2003, Jack Layton was presented with a plan for a merger of the NDP with the Canadian Action Party and the embryonic new Alternative Party, led by Gilles Lavoie of Alma, Québec, to form the nucleus of a big new, broadly-based, progressive pro-Canada party. I would like to underline the word nucleus because this "doable" merger would only be the beginning. There are literally thousands of David Orchard supporters and other "progressive" Conservatives who are ready to climb on the bandwagon. If my e-mail is a reliable barometer of interest, there would also be large numbers of patriots from the Alliance and Liberal Party looking for a vehicle to save their beloved country.

Mail from Québec leads me to believe that there could be surprising support from that province as well. Increasingly, thoughtful Québecers are coming to realize that corporate globalization rather than federalism is the greatest threat to the French language and French-Canadian culture in North America. Their security depends on a strong Québec within a strong and independent Canada.

The key move is the first one. Jack Layton has to accept the merger proposed and sell it to his supporters. That would facilitate the three essentials for success – a new name, a new constitution, and a new image based on the new reality. These three would provide the new party with the rocket-assisted boost necessary to propel it out front, ahead of the pack, as the government's number one challenger. Then every Canadian would have to choose which he or she loved the most – their party or their country.

Jack Layton knows in his heart what has to be done. He has to overcome the opposition of "conservatives" in his own party. He will also have to overcome the resistance of those who think that "movements" can move mountains. They may move mountains but they can't win elections and abrogate treaties. Only parties can, and only the most naïve NDPer would believe that they could do it on their own.

To light the fuse for the rocket launch requires an early and unequivocal commitment from Jack Layton. It will be the ultimate test of his vision for what is required and possible for Canada. The difference between the possible and impossible is a measure of a person's will.

As U.S. President Harry S. Truman said: "Men make history, and not the other way around. In periods where there is no leadership, society stands still. Progress occurs when courageous, skillful leaders seize the opportunity to change things for the better."

If Jack's answer is yes, he will be applauded and supported. If, heaven forbid, he should say no, or dither until it is too late, history will attest to the opportunity lost.

TO ENCOURAGE JACK LAYTON TO ACT

   e-mail: jack@fed.ndp.ca
Post mail: Mr. Jack Layton, Leader
              New Democratic Party of Canada
              1001-75 Albert Street
              Ottawa, Ontario   K1P 5E7
     Fax: (613) 230-9950

TO CONTACT PAUL HELLYER

   e-mail: phellyer@canadianactionparty.ca
Post mail: Hon. Paul Hellyer, Leader
              Canadian Action Party
              302 – 99 Atlantic Ave.
              Toronto, ON M6K 3J8
     Fax: (416) 535-6325

TO REGISTER YOUR SUPPORT FOR ONE BIG PARTY

   URL: www.onebigparty.ca

NOTES

Chapter 1: From One Evil Empire to Another

1. Lind, Michael, "The Weird Men Behind George W. Bush's War," New Statesman, April 12, 2003.
2. "American Century," Pentagon Document on Post-Cold-War Strategy, February 18, 1992.
3. As reported in the New York Times, May 24, 1992.
4. Ibid.
5. "Rebuilding America's Defenses: Strategy, Forces and Resources For a New Century, A Report of The Project for the New American Century, September 2000.
6. From the text of U.S. President George W. Bush's address to a joint meeting of Congress, September 20, 2001.
7. From a translated text of Osama bin Laden's broadcast taken from the *New York Times*, October 8, 2001.
8. Excerpt from an article by Barrie McKenna, "Bush faces furor over knowledge of attack," *Globe and Mail*, May 17, 2002.
9. Chossudovsky, Michel, *War and Globalisation: The Truth Behind September 11*. Shanty Bay, Ontario: Global Outlook, 2002.
10. Excerpt from an article by Michele Landsberg, "Conspiracy crusader doubts official 9/11 version," *Toronto Star*, May 11, 2003.

Chapter 2: The War on Iraq

1. As reported in *World Tribune*, Middle East Newsline, December 20, 2001.
2. Excerpt from an article by Kevin Donovan, "How Saddam plotted to get A-bomb power," *Toronto Star*, January 31, 2003.
3. A Report of Chairman Donald W. Riegle, Jr. and Ranking Member Alfonse M. D'Amato of the Committee on Banking, Housing and Urban Affairs with Respect to Export Administration, United States Senate, 103rd Congress, 2nd Session, May 25, 1994.
4. *Ibid.*
5. Excerpt from an article by Estanislo Oziewicz, "United Nations weapons inspectors weren't thrown out of Iraq," *Globe and Mail*, April 4, 2003.
6. Excerpt from an article by Vilip Hiro, "When US turned a blind eye to poison gas," *The Observer*, September 1, 2002.
7. Scott Ritter speaking in London, England to CNN's Fionnuala Sweeney, July 17, 2002.
8. *Ibid.*
9. Source: *Encyclopedia Americana*.
10. Excerpt from an article by David E. Sanger, "N. Korea admits it has nuclear weapons," *Toronto Star*, April 23, 2003.
11. CBC Radio, "As it Happens," May 12, 2003.
12. *Ibid.*
13. *Ibid.*

14. Defense Planning Guidance on Post-Cold-War Strategy, February 1992 and subsequent revisions including the one of September 2000.

15. "Plans for Iraq Attack Began on 9/11", as reported on CBS News, September 4, 2002

16. Excerpt from an article by Laura King, "1,700 Baghdadis died in war, analysis says," *Toronto Star*, May 18, 2003.

17. Editorial, "Free Fall in Iraq," *New York Times*, May 8, 2003.

18. Excerpt from an article by Gloria Galloway, "U.S. rebukes Canada," *Globe and Mail*, March 26, 2003.

19. "Joint Plan Red" by Thaddeus Holt in the Quarterly Journal of Military History, Autumn 1988, Vol. 1, No. 1, p. 48.

Chapter 3: American Values and Interests

1. Lapham, Lewis, "Pax Iconomica," in *Behind the Headlines*, Vol. 54, No. 2, Winter 1996-97, p. 9 in his 'On Politics, Culture and Media' keynote address to the Canadian Institute of International Affairs national foreign policy conference in October, 1996.

2. *Ibid.*, p. 8.

3. Memorandum E-A10, 19 October, 1940, CFR, War-Peace Studies, Baldwin Papers, Box 117.

4. Memorandum T-A25, 20 May, 1942, CFR, War-Peace Studies, Hoover Library on War, Revolution and Peace.

5. The first meeting of the elite group was held at the Hotel de Bilderberg, Holland, in May 1954 under the chairmanship of Prince Bernhard of the Netherlands. It has met every year since with one exception.

6. "The Crisis of Democracy: Report on the Governability of Democracies to the Trilateral Commission," 1975.

7. Sklar, Holly (ed.), *Trilateralism: The Trilateral Commission and Elite Planning for World Management*. Boston: South End Press, 1980.

8. Source: Center for Responsive Politics, Washington, D.C.   (N.B. Additional details are available from their website.)

9. *Ibid.*

10. *Ibid.*

11. Source: *Forbes* magazine, April 24, 2003.

12. Peter G. Peterson, Chairman of the Council on Foreign Relations, his address, jointly sponsored by the Canadian Institute of International Affairs and the Ramsay Luncheon Series, October 29, 2002.

13. Excerpt from an article by Barrie McKenna, "Enron's Lay snubs Congress," *Globe and Mail*, February 4, 2002.

14. Excerpt from an article by Stephen Labaton, "MCI Agrees to Pay $500 Million in Fraud Case," *New York Times*, May 20. 2003.

15. *Ibid.*

16. Excerpt from an article by Stephen Labaton, "10 Wall St. Firms Settle with U.S. in Analyst Inquiry," *New York Times*, April 29, 2003.

17. Excerpt from an article by Brian Miller, "There's little repentance on Wall Street these days," *Globe and Mail*, April 28, 2003.

18. Editorial, "Wall Street Revisionism," *New York Times*, May 1, 2003.

19. Excerpt from an article by Stephen Labaton, "Wall St. settlement: 10 Wall St. firms reach settlement in analyst inquiry," *New York Times*, April 29, 2003.

20. Excerpt from an article by David Wessel, "Market Bubble Magnified Shifts in Business Mores," *Globe and Mail*, June 20, 2002.
21. Excerpt from an article by Sandra Rubin, "Have we cleaned up our own act? Forget it," *Financial Post*, July 13, 2002.

Chapter 4: A Compass in Need of Repair

1. "A Prayer for America," Dennis Kucinich in a speech to the Southern California Americans for Democratic Action, in Los Angeles, on February 17, 2002.
2. Article II, Section I, of the United States' Constitution.
3. Editorial, "In the Aftermath of Sept. 11," *New York Times*, May 23, 2003.
4. *Ibid.*
5. Editorial, "US plans death camp," *The Courier-Mail*, May 26, 2003.
6. *Ibid.*
7. Excerpt from an article by Jan Cienski, "War was not about WMDs: Wolfowitz," *National Post*, May 30, 2003.
8. *Ibid.*
9. Excerpt from an article by Dalton Camp, "Free speech has become war casualty," *Toronto Star*, October 14, 2001.
10. Excerpt from an article by Vit Wagner, "Outspoken Earl warns of these dangerous times," *Toronto Star*, May 16, 2003.
11. *Ibid.*
12. CBS news report, "Talkin' Pensions and Politics," March 1, 2002.
13. Excerpt from an article by David Olive, "A slap on the wrist is a joke for these capital crimes," *Toronto Star*, May 1, 2003.
14. Excerpt from an article by Warren Richey, "High court Oks 'three strikes' law," *Christian Science Monitor*, March 6, 2003.
15. *Ibid.*
16. Excerpt from an article by Robert Pear, "New Study Finds 60 Million Uninsured During a Year," New York Times, May 13, 2003.
17. *Ibid.*
18. The couple were Tom and Barbara Skinner. He died June 17, 1994.
19. Excerpt from an article by Robin Toner and Robert Pear, "Cutbacks Emperil Health Coverage for States' Poor," *New York Times*, April 28, 2003.
20. Excerpt from an article by Robert Pear, "Plan to Overhaul Medicare by Enlarging Private Health Plan Role is Criticized," *New York Times*, May 6, 2003.
21. Excerpt from an article by David Olive, "Profits and hospitals don't mix," *Toronto Star*, April 26, 2003.
22. Editorial, "The Republicans Party On," *New York Times*, May 22, 2003.
23. Excerpt from an article by Robert J. Shiller, "Mind the Gap," New York Times, May 15, 2003.
24. *Ibid.*
25. *Ibid.*
26. Editorial, "Papers Show Expanded Halliburton Iraq Role," *New York Times*, May 6, 2003.
27. *Ibid.*
28. Excerpt from an article by Bob Herbert, "Dancing With the Devil," *New York Times*, May 22, 2003.

29. *Ibid.*

Chapter 5: Leadership Lost

1. Source: Center for Defense Information, 2001-2002 Military Almanac.
2. *New York Times*, editorial, "'Little Bitty', More's the Pity," April 28, 2003.
3. Hjertholm, Peter and White, Howard: *Foreign aid in historical perspective: Background and trends.* London: Routledge, 2000.
4. Caldicott, Helen: *The New Nuclear Danger: George W. Bush's Military-Industrial Complex.* New York: The New Press, 2002, pp. 2-3.
5. "Rebuilding America's Defenses: Strategy, Forces and Resources For a New Century," A Report of The Project for the New American Century, September 2000.
6. *Ibid.*
7. Excerpt from an article by Peronet Despeignes, "U.S. Facing Deficit of US$44-trillion," *National Post*, May 29, 2003.
8. *Ibid.*
9. Bible: Matthew 23, Verse 27.
10. Bible: Psalm 137, Verses 8-9.
11. McLaughlin, Abraham, "How far Americans would go to fight terror," *Christian Science Monitor*, November 14, 2001.
12. *Ibid.*
13. "The National Security Strategy of the United States of America," The White House, Washington, D.C., September 20, 2002.
14. Sen. Edward M. Kennedy, "The Bush Doctrine of Pre-Emption," *Congressional Record,* October 7, 2002.
15. *Ibid.*
16. Caldicott, Helen, *"The New Nuclear Danger,"* p.4
17. *Ibid.*
18. Report by Reuters, "U.S. Nuclear Aims Raise Arms – Control Fears," June 1, 2003.
19. *Ibid.*
20. Statement by the President, "President Announces Progress in Missile Defense Capabilities," December 17, 2002.
21. "Rebuilding America's Defenses."
22. *Ibid.*
23. *Ibid.*
24. Maj. Gen. Franklin J. Blaisdell, Air Force Briefing on "Space: The Warfighter's Perspective," March 12, 2003.
25. *Ibid.*
26. Caldicott, Helen, *"The New Nuclear Danger,"* p.5

Chapter 6: Wall Street and the Axis of Evil

1. Gregory Palast in an interview with *Acres USA*, June 2003.
2. George, Susan, "Winning the War of Ideas: Lessons from the Gramscian Right," originally published in *Dissent*, Summer 1997.
3. *Ibid.*
4. Joseph, Stiglitz E., *Globalization and its Discontents.* New York: Norton Trade, April 2003, p. 71.
5. Finnegan, William, "The Economics of Empire: Notes on the Washington Consensus," published in *Harper's* magazine, May, 2003.

6. An excerpt from an article by Gregory Palast, "Failures of the 20th Century: See Under I.M.F.," *The London Observer*, October 8, 2000.
7. Finnegan, William, "The Economics of Empire."
8. "World Bank Secret Documents Consumes Argentina," Gregory Palast in an interview with Alex Jones, March 4, 2002.
9. *Ibid.*
10. *Ibid.*
11. Joseph Stiglitz E., *Globalization and its Discontents*, p.231.
12. Economic Report of the President, 1991, 1994 and OECD.
13. Source: OECD.
14. Palast, Gregory, "Failures of the 20th Century."
15. Finnegan, William, "The Economics of Empire."
16. Lester, Richard A., "Currency Issues to Overcome Depressions in Pennsylvania, 1723 and 1729," *The Journal of Political Economy*, Vol. 46, June 1938, p. 338.
17. Smith, Adam, *Wealth of Nations*. New York: P.F. Collier and Son, 1909, p. 266.
18. Remarks by Soros, George, "The Crisis of Global Capitalism: Open Society Endangered," December 10, 1998.

Chapter 7: Where Does Money Comes From?

1. Galbraith, J.K., *Money, Whence it Came, Where it Went*. Boston: Houghton Mifflin Company, 1975, p. 18.
2. Hixson, William F., *Triumph of the Bankers: Money and Banking in the Eighteenth and Nineteenth Centuries*. Westport: Praeger Publishers, 1993, p. 46.
3. Sources: Bank of Canada Report, "The Transmission of Monetary Policy in Canada," 1996. *The Canadian Banker*, Vol. 106, No. 5, Sept-Oct, 1999.
4. An excerpt from an article by William Keegan, "So Now Friedman Says He Was Wrong," *The Observer*, June 22, 2003.

Chapter 8: The Banks Play Monopoly

1. Bank of Canada Review, Summer 1997, p. 47 and Bank of Canada Weekly Financial Statistics, June 30, 2003.
2. An excerpt from an article by Derek DeCloet, "How CIBC keeps money from the taxman," *Financial Post*, February 23, 2002.
3. Source: *The Banker*, July 2002.
4. *Ibid.*
5. Lead editorial, "Canadian banks need size to compete internationally," *Financial Post* , August 12, 1996.
6. As reported in the *Toronto Star*, October 3, 1996.
7. Lead editorial, "Carve up the sacred cow of bank ownership," *Globe and Mail*, June 20, 1997.
8. Bank of Montreal "Policy Alternatives for Canadian Financial Services," July 1997.
9. Excerpt from an article by John Partridge and Susanne Craig, "Banks drop $40-billion bombshell", *Globe and Mail*, January 24, 1998.
10. An excerpt from an article by Simon Tuck and Paul Waldie, "Manley stokes merger hopes," *Globe and Mail*, October 25, 2002.

11. An excerpt from an article by Rob Ferguson and Tim Harper, "Manley bids to restart bank mergers debate," *Toronto Star*, October 25, 2002.

12. *Ibid.*

13. Editorial, "Banks and the public," *Toronto Star*, October 27, 2002.

14. An excerpt from an article by Jacquie McNish and John Partridge, "Banks were set to seal merger," *Globe and Mail*, October 30, 2002.

15. An excerpt from an article by Sinclair Stewart, "Put no limit on mergers or ban all: TD boss," *Globe and Mail*, March 5, 2003.

16. An excerpt from an article by Simon Tuck, "Big changes seen ahead for banks," *Globe and Mail*, October 28, 2002.

17. Source: Royal Bank Annual Statement, 2002, p. 98.

18. Source: Bank of Montreal, 180th Annual Report, 1997.

19. As reported in the *Globe and Mail*, May 31, 2003.

Chapter 9: Mulroney's Sizzle is a Fizzle

1. Excerpt from an article by Kevin Cox, "Praise for free trade is long overdue, Mulroney declares," *Globe and Mail*, May 29, 2002.

2. Excerpt from an article by Shawn McCarthy, "Large majority backs free trade," *Globe and Mail*, June 9, 2003.

3. Source: National Farmers Union, 2717 Wentz Ave., Saskatoon, SK S7K 4B6. (For source of individual items contact NFU.)

4. *Ibid.*

5. Excerpt from an article by Maude Barlow, "Washington to Canada: Fill 'er Up," *Globe and Mail*, September 26, 2000.

6. Based on Michael B. Smith's recollection of the meeting aboard Smith's 34-foot Sabre Sloop, *Wind*, as recorded in *Building a Partnership: The Canada-United States Free Trade Agreement*, Mordechai Kreinin (ed.). East Lansing: Michigan State University Press, 2001, p. 7.

7. Excerpt from an article by John Saunders, "U.S. hits Canada with duties on durum, red spring wheat," *Globe and Mail*, May 5, 2003.

8. As reported in the *Vancouver Sun*, January 12, 2000.

9. As reported in the *National Post*, March 2, 2002.

10. Excerpt from an article by Steve Maich and Paul Vieira, "U.S. firm eyes bid for Air Canada," *National Post*, July 8, 2003.

11. Hurtig, Mel, *The Vanishing Country: Is it too late to save Canada?* Toronto: McClelland & Stewart Ltd., 2002, pp. 52-53.

12. MacArthur, John R., *The Selling of "Free Trade": NAFTA, Washington and the Subversion of American Democracy*. New York: Hill and Wang, 2000.

13. Commission for Environmental Cooperation, "The North American Mosaic: A State of the Environment Report, 2001.

14. Editorial, "High-priced growth," *Toronto Star*, January 8, 2002.

15. *Ibid.*

16. Excerpt from an article by Linda McQuaig, "U.S. wants to liberate our energy," *Toronto Star*, April 20, 2003.

17. Excerpt from an article by Kelly Toughill, "Natural gas fight fuels nationalist fire," *Toronto Star*, July 13, 2002.

18. McQuaig, Linda, "U.S. wants to liberate our energy."

19. Excerpt from an article by Kevin Cox, "Praise for free trade is long overdue, Mulroney declares," op. cit.

20. Dungan, P. and S. Murphy, "The Changing Industry and Skill Mix of Canada's International Trade," *Perspective on North American Free Trade*, Paper No. 4, Industry Canada, 1999.
21. Campbell, Bruce, "False Promise: Canada in the Free Trade Era," EPI Briefing Paper, April 2001.

Chapter 10: Defence and Foreign Policy

1. Plomer, James, "The Gold-braid Mind is Destroying Our Navy," *Maclean's* magazine, September 7, 1963.
2. From a conversation between Bill Lee, my executive assistant, and one of the researchers employed by the commission.
3. Bland, Douglas, *The Administration of Defense Policy in Canada 1947 to 1985*, Kingston: Ronald P. Frye & Co., 1987, p. 81.
4. An excerpt from an article by Lewis MacKenzie, "Lewis MacKenzie: On choosing a Chief of Defense Staff, *Globe and Mail*, May 27, 1996.
5. J.L. Granatstein, "A Friendly Agreement in Advance: Canada-US Defense Relations Past, Present, and Future." C.D. Howe Institute, The Border Papers, No. 166, June 2002.
6. "Rebuilding America's Defenses: Strategy, Forces and Resources For a New Century, A Report of The Project for the New American Century, September 2000.

Chapter 11: A World of Hope

1. Ritter, Scott, *Frontier Justice: Weapons of Mass Destruction and the Bushwhacking of America*. Context Books, 2003.
2. Address by Congressman Ron Paul of Texas, "Neo-CONNED!" July 10, 2003 (http://www.house.gov/paul/openingpage.htm).
3. *Ibid.*
4. Stiglitz, Joseph E., *Globalization and Its Discontents*. New York: Norton Trade, 2003.
5. Shaefer, Standard, "Duck, Duck, Goose: Financing the War, Financing the World," April 23, 2003.
6. Thomas, William, "The Bucks Stop Here," Lifeboatnews.com
7. *Ibid.*
8. *Ibid.*
9. Source: International Financial Statistics Yearbook, 2002.
10. "Publicly Created Money and Monetary Reform," is the title of Early Day Motion 854, tabled by David Chaytor, MP in the House of Commons, March 20, 2003.

Chapter 12: Why Paul Martin Won't Do

1. Letter to Prime Minister Jean Chrétien, October 28, 1993
2. Letter to Paul Martin, October 28, 1993.
3. Editorial, "Mulroney First in Class, Chrétien Last," *Globe and Mail* Supplement, June 2001
4. An excerpt from an article by Edward Greenspon, "What was the extent of the budget cut?" *Globe and Mail*, February 17, 1999.
5. An excerpt from an article by Carolyn Abraham and Lisa Priest, "Cutbacks fed SARS calamity, critics say," *Globe and Mail*, May 3, 2003.

6.   *Ibid.*
7.   An excerpt from an article by Theresa Boyle, "Food safety branded 'critical'," *Toronto Star*, November 30, 2001.
8.   *Ibid.*
9.   An excerpt from an article by Deborah Yedlin, "Meat testing backlog created by cutbacks," *Globe and Mail*, May 23, 2003.
10. An excerpt from an article by Richard Brennan and Nicolaas van Rijn, "Walkerton 'could have been prevented'," *Toronto Star*, January 19, 2002.
11. *Ibid.*
12. An excerpt from an article by Kevin Donovan, "Bad water reports soaring," *Toronto Star*, May 17, 2003.
13. Access 2000, Canadian Federation of Students Fact Sheet.
14. An excerpt from an article by David Leblanc, "Wing cracks ground nine aging Hercules," *Globe and Mail*, April 18, 2003.
15. *Ibid.*
16. Editorial, "There's no cheap fix for Toronto gridlock." *Toronto Star*, August 15, 2002.
17. An excerpt from an article by Caroline Alphonso, "Schools to levy fees for field, equipment use," *Globe and Mail*, February 8, 2003.
18. Editorial, "School fees hurt kids," *Toronto Star*, May 22, 2003.
19. Paul Martin, in a speech given to a luncheon organized by the Reinventing Bretton Woods Committee, and the Conference Board of Canada, in Ottawa entitled "Globalization, Terrorism and the World Economy," November 16, 2001.
20. *Ibid.*
21. An excerpt from an article by Shawn McCarthy, "Martin promises to repair U.S. ties," *Globe and Mail*, April 26, 2003.
22. An excerpt from an article by Les Whittington, "He's in the money," *Toronto Star*, July 19, 2003.
23. *Ibid.*
24. *Ibid.*

Chapter 13: A Real Northern Tiger

1.   An excerpt from an article by Alan Toulin, "New Kyoto proposal draws fire," *Financial Post*, March 7, 2002.
2.   An excerpt from an article by Martin Mitelstaedt, "Ottawa targeted for mine cleanups," *Globe and Mail*, October 22, 2002.
3.   An excerpt from an article by Peter Calamai, "Nuclear cleanup to cost billions," *Toronto Star*, April 11, 2003.
4.   An excerpt from an article by Kerry Gillespie, "Tolls coming, planner says," *Toronto Star*, June 6, 2003.
5.   *Ibid.*
6.   *Ibid.*
7.   Editorial, "Feds plan $3B fix for railways," *Toronto Sun*, August 4, 2002.
8.   Editorial, "Can Canada's surplus survive harder times," *Globe and Mail*, June 19. 2003.
9.   Andrew Jackson, senior economist, Canadian Labour Congress, in a letter to Richard Priestman dated July 16, 2003.
10. *Toronto Star*, "Royal Bank backs bit for Selfridges," June 12, 2003.

APPENDIX A

The Bush Doctrine of Pre-Emption

By Sen. Edward M. Kennedy

October 7, 2002

We face no more serious decision in our democracy than whether or not to go to war. The American people deserve to fully understand all of the implications of such a decision.

The question of whether our nation should attack Iraq is playing out in the context of a more fundamental debate that is only just beginning – an all-important debate about how, when and where in the years ahead our country will use its unsurpassed military might.

On September 20, the Administration unveiled its new National Security Strategy. This document addresses the new realities of our age, particularly the proliferation of weapons of mass destruction and terrorist networks armed with the agendas of fanatics. The Strategy claims that these new threats are so novel and so dangerous that we should "not hesitate to act alone, if necessary, to exercise our right of self-defense by acting pre-emptively."

But in the discussion over the past few months about Iraq, the Administration, often uses the terms "pre-emptive" and "preventive" interchangeably. In the realm of international relations, these two terms have long had very different meanings.

Traditionally, "pre-emptive" action refers to times when states react to an imminent threat of attack. For example, when Egyptian and Syrian forces mobilized on Israel's borders in 1967, the threat was obvious and immediate, and Israel felt justified in pre-emptively attaching those forces. The global community is generally tolerant of such actions, since no nation should have to suffer a certain strike before it has the legitimacy to respond.

By contrast, "preventive" military action refers to strikes that target a country before it has developed a capability that could someday become threatening. Preventive attacks have generally been condemned. For example, the 1941 sneak attack on Pearl Harbor was regarded as a preventive strike by Japan, because the Japanese were seeking to block a planned military buildup by the United States in the Pacific.

The coldly premeditated nature of preventive attacks and preventive wars makes them anathema to well-established international principles against aggression. Pearl Harbor has been rightfully recorded in history as an act of dishonorable treachery.

Historically, the United States has condemned the idea of preventive war, because it violates basic international rules against aggression. But at times in our history, preventive war has been seriously advocated as a policy option.

In the early days of the Cold War, some U.S. military and civilian experts advocated a preventive war against the Soviet Union. They proposed a devastating first strike to prevent the Soviet Union from developing a threatening nuclear capability. At the time, they said the uniquely destructive power of nuclear weapons required us to rethink traditional international rules.

The first round of that debate ended in 1950, when President Truman ruled out a preventive strike, stating that such actions were not consistent with our American tradition. He said, "You don't 'prevent' anything by war ... except peace." Instead of a surprise first strike, the nation dedicated itself to the strategy of deterrence and containment, which successfully kept the peace during the long and frequently difficult years of the Cold War.

Arguments for preventive war resurfaced again when the Eisenhower Administration took power in 1953, but President Eisenhower and Secretary of State John Foster Dulles soon decided firmly against it. President Eisenhower emphasized that even if we were to win such a war, we would face the vast burdens of occupation and reconstruction that would come with it.

The argument that the United States should take preventive military action, in the absence of an imminent attack, resurfaced in 1962, when we learned that the Soviet Union would soon have the ability to launch missiles from Cuba against our country. Many military officers urged President Kennedy to approve a preventive attack to destroy this capability before it became operational. Robert Kennedy, like Harry Truman, felt that this kind of first strike was not consistent with American values. He said that a proposed surprise first strike against Cuba would be a Pearl Harbor in reverse. "For 175 years," he said, "we have not been that kind of country." That view prevailed. A middle ground was found and peace was preserved.

Yet another round of debate followed the Cuban Missile Crisis when American strategists and voices in and out of the Administration advocated preventive wars against China to forestall its acquisition of nuclear weapons. Many arguments heard today about Iraq were made then about the Chinese communist government; that its leadership was irrational and that it was therefore undeterrable. And once again, those arguments were rejected.

As these earlier cases show, American strategic thinkers have long debated the relative merits of preventive and pre-emptive war. Although nobody would deny our right to pre-emptively block an imminent attack on our territory, there is disagreement about our right to preventively engage in war.

In each of these cases a way was found to deter other nations, without waging war.

Now, the Bush Administration says we must take pre-emptive action against Iraq. But what the Administration is really calling for is preventive war, which flies in the face of international rules of acceptable behaviour. The Administration's new National Security Strategy states "As a matter of common sense and self-defense, America will act against such emerging threats before they are fully formed."

The circumstances of today's world require us to rethink this concept. The world changed on September 11th, and all of us have learned that it can be a drastically more dangerous place. The Bush Administration's new National Security Strategy asserts that global realities now legitimize preventive war and make it a strategic necessity.

The document openly contemplates preventive attacks against groups or states, even absent the threat of imminent attack. It legitimizes this kind of first strike option, and it elevates it to the status of a core security doctrine. Disregarding norms of international behavior, the Bush Strategy asserts that the United States should be exempt from the rules we expect other nations to obey.

I strongly oppose any such extreme doctrine and I'm sure that many others do so as well. Earlier generations of Americans rejected preventive war on the grounds of both morality and practicality, and our generation must do so as well. We can deal with Iraq without resorting to this extreme.

It is impossible to justify any such double standard under international law. Might does not make right. America cannot write its own rules for the modern world. To attempt to do so would be unilateralism run amok. It would antagonize our closest allies, whose support we need to fight terrorism, prevent global warming, and deal with many other dangers that affect all nations and require international cooperation. It would deprive America of the moral legitimacy necessary to promote our values abroad. And it would give other nations – from Russia to India to Pakistan – an excuse to violate fundamental principles of civilized international behavior.

The Administration's doctrine is a call for 21st century American imperialism that no nation can or should accept. It is the antithesis of all that America has worked so hard to achieve in international relations since the end of World War II.

This is not just an academic debate. There are important real world consequences. A shift in our policy toward preventive war would reinforce the perception of America as a "bully" in the Middle East, and would fuel anti-American sentiment throughout the Islamic world an beyond.

It would also send a signal to governments the world over that the rules of aggression have changed for them too, which could increase the risk of conflict between countries such as Russia and Georgia, India and Pakistan, and China and Taiwan.

Obviously, this debate is only just beginning on the Administration's new strategy for national security. But the debate is solidly grounded in American values and history.

It will also be a debate among vast numbers of well-meaning Americans who have honest differences of opinion about the best way to use U.S. military might. The debate will be contentious, but the stakes – in terms of both our national security and our allegiance to our core beliefs – are too high to ignore. I look forward to working closely with my colleagues in Congress to develop an effective and principled policy that will enable us to protect our national security and respect the basic principles that are essential for the world to be at peace.

Senator Edward M. Kennedy represents Massachusetts in the United States Senate.

BIBLIOGRAPHY

Caldicott, Helen. *The New Nuclear Danger: George W. Bush's Military-Industrial Complex.* NY: The New Press, 2002.

Caufield, Catherine, *Masters of Illusion: The World Bank and the Poverty of Nations*, New York: Henry Holt and Company, 1996.

Chossudovsky, Michel, *War and Globalisation: The Truth Behind September 11.* Shanty Bay, Ontario: Global Outlook, 2002.

Danaher, Kevin (ed.), *50 Years is Enough: The Case Against the World Bank and the International Monetary Fund*, Boston: South End Press, 1994.

Finnegan, William, "The Economics of Empire: Notes on the Washington Consensus," published in *Harper's* magazine, May, 2003.

Galbraith, J.K., *Money, Whence it Came, Where it Went.* Boston: Houghton Mifflin Company, 1975.

Hellyer, Paul, *Surviving the Global Financial Crisis: The Economics of Hope for Generation X.* Toronto: Chimo Media, 1996.

Hellyer, Paul, *Goodbye Canada.* Toronto: Chimo Media, 2001.

Hixson, William F., *Triumph of the Bankers: Money and Banking in the Eighteenth and Nineteenth Centuries.* Westport: Praeger Publishers, 1993.

Hurtig, Mel, *The Vanishing Country: Is it too late to save Canada?* Toronto: McClelland & Stewart Ltd., 2002.

MacArthur, John R., *The Selling of "Free Trade": NAFTA, Washington and the Subversion of American Democracy.* New York: Hill and Wang, 2000.

Palast, Gregory, *The Best Democracy Money Can Buy*, New York: Plume, 2003.

Sklar, Holly (ed.), *Trilateralism: The Trilateral Commission and Elite Planning for World Management.* Boston: South End Press, 1980.

Ritter, Scott, Frontier Justice: *Weapons of Mass Destruction and the Bushwhacking of America.* Context Books, 2003.

Stiglitz, Joseph, E., *Globalization and its Discontents.* New York: Norton Trade, 2003.

INDEX

A

Acton , Lord, 24
agriculture *see* farmers and free trade
Alaska boundary dispute, 20-21
Alexander, Nancy, 69
Allen, Elyse, 174
Allende, Salvador, 17
Alliance, 180
Alternative Party, 183
American Enterprise Institute, 64
Andrade case, 41-42
annexation by U.S., 179
Argentina, 60-71
armed forces, Canadian, 124-134
   "civilianization" a mistake, 134
   collaboration with U.S., 135-138
   concerns and goals, 171
   effects of cutbacks, 161
   peacekeeping, 139-140
   present needs, 135
   story of unification, 125-133
   see also military buildup in U.S.
arts
   concerns and goals, 175
   effects of cutbacks, 159
assassinations, 53
Atkinson, Lloyd, 98
atomic weapons *see* nuclear weapons
automotive trade with U.S., 104
Axworthy, Lloyd, 139

B

Baillie, Charles, 92
Bank Act (amended 1991), 79, 82,
   85, 87-88, 177
Bank for International Settlements,
   151
Bank for Reconstruction and
   Development *see* World Bank
Bank of Canada, 79, 81, 170-172
   and recession of 1980s, 171
   in World War II, 176
Bank of England, 80
Bank of Montreal, 93-94, 95, 96,
   100

banks
   central banks, 68, 72, 81, 149
   creation of money, 78-79, 80, 81-
      84, 98, 151, 171-172
   and developing countries, 68, 152-
      153
   expansion of Canadian banks into
      U.S., 115
   loans to entrepreneurs, 99-100
   mergers, 92-102
   microbanking, 99
   monopolizing financial services,
      87-91, 102
   reserve requirements, 79-80
Barlow, Maude, 111
Barnes, Sue, 97
Barrett, Matthew, 93
Bay Street, 33
Berlin Wall, 2
Berridge, Joe, 174
Bilderbergers, 26
bin Laden , Osama, 8, 53, 54
biological warfare, 12-13
Blair, Tony, 14-15
Blaisdell, Franklin J., 59-60
Bolivia, 69-70
bonds, government, 82, 84
Bouey, Gerald, 79, 171
Bowman , Isaiah, 26
brainwashing, 11, 17-18, 38, 97
   globalization, 62-63
   war on Iraq, 11, 17-18, 38
Bremer, Paul, 19
Bretton Woods Conference, 67
Brooks , Leonard, 33
Brzezinski, Zbigniew, 27
Bush, George W., 6, 7, 43, 44, 46
   and Iraq war, 11-12, 15, 16, 141
   military buildup, 49-50, 52, 54, 57
   and New World Order, 62, 66, 70,
      72
   and religious right, 52-53
   and terrorism, 8-9, 40

C

Caccia, Charles, 118

Caldicott , Helen, 49, 60
campaign funds for Paul Martin, 165
campaign funds in U.S., 28-29
Campbell, Bruce, 121
Canada Council, 162
Canadian Action Party, 166, 183
"capital adequacy" for banks, 83-84
Carter , Jimmy, 28
CBC, 163, 175
Cellucci , Paul, 20, 141
central banks, 68, 72, 81, 149
Chamberlain , Neville, 15
chemical warfare, 13
Cheney , Dick, 3, 6
Chossudovsky , Michel, 9, 149
church and state, 52-54
CIA, 17, 35
civilian deaths in Iraq war, 19
classical economists, 76
Clinton , Bill, 49, 115
Cold War, 1, 22
collateral, 82, 85
Commonwealth, 140
compensation , executive, 30
Competition Bureau, 93-97, 170
concerns and goals
    affordable housing, 173
    armed forces, arts, 175
    education, 172-173
    environment, 173
    farmers, 171
    fishermen, 175
    health care, 172
    infrastructure, 174
    transportation, 174
constitutional rights in U.S., 34-36,
    39-40
corporate culture in U.S. and
    Canada, 30-33
corporations vs. nations, 116
Council on Foreign Relations (U.S.),
    23, 26-27
Crow, John, 159, 170
"crowding out," 178
currency, 64, 73-74
    new world currency proposed,
    148-151, 155
cutbacks in 1995 budget, 159-165
    arts, environment, 162
    defence, infrastructure, 163
    education, 161-162, 164

health care, 159-161

D

defence see armed forces, Canadian
democracy lost with globalization,
    145-146
developing countries
    in Cold War period, 2
    effects of globalization, 64-71,
        144-145
    elimination of debt, 151-153, 155
dictators, 16-17
Disraeli, Benjamin, 34
Dixie Chicks, 39
Dodge, David, 159, 170, 177
Donaldson , William, 41-42
Dorgan , Byron, 31
double standards in U.S., 40-42, 45-
    46, 56, 58
    economic inequality, 45
    health care, 43-44
    justice, 40-42
    preventive wars, 55-60
    transparency or secrecy, 46-47
downloading of fiscal responsibility,
    159, 165
Dumping and Anti-Subsidy laws,
    U.S., 111-112
Dungan and Murphy study, 120

E

Earle , Steve, 39
East Asia meltdown, 98
economic fundamentalism, 68-74,
    147, 171-172, 173
Economist, The, 177
Edison, Thomas, 177
education
    concerns and goals, 172-173
    effects of cutbacks, 159-160, 162
Eisenhower , Dwight D., 11
election process in U.S., 28-29
electronic money, 80
elite in U.S., 29, 31-33, 65
empire-building by U.S., 58, 62-63
energy security, NAFTA, 118
Enron Corporation, 31, 70
entrepreneurs and bank loans, 99-100
environment
    concerns and goals, 173
    effects of cutbacks, 161
    and NAFTA, 117

Euro, 148-150
Ewing case, 41
exports and imports see free trade

F

farmers
    concerns and goals, 175
    and free trade, 105-111
Farris , Stephen, 53
FBI, 35
Federal Reserve System in U.S., 79,
    152
Financial Post, 93
financial services monopolized by
    banks, 87-91, 101
Finnegan, William, 67, 70, 73
first strike capability, 59, 139
fishermen, 175-176
food supply, safety, 159-160
foreign aid, 51-52, 53-54
Foreign Investment Review Board,
    112, 114
foreign ownership, 97, 99, 111, 112-
    115
foreign policy of Canada, 136-137
"fractional reserve" system of
    banking, 78
France, 15, 38
Francophonie, 141
Franklin, Benjamin, 73
fraud in U.S. firms, 31-33, 40-41
free trade, 66-67, 72, 102-123
    automotive trade with U.S., 103,
        105
    Canadian vs. U.S. income, 120-
        121
    energy exports to U.S., 103-104,
        119
    negative aspects for farmers, 105-
        111
    sale of Canadian companies, 114-
        115
    score card, 123
    and unemployment, 119-120
    see also Free Trade Agreement;
        globalization; NAFTA
Free Trade Agreement, 22, 28, 102,
    123
    supported by PCs, 180
    U.S. gains advantage, 111-114
freedom of expression, 39-40

Friedman, Milton, 62, 67, 68, 73,
    78-79, 84, 86
fundamentalist economics *see*
    economic fundamentalism
Future Years Defense Program, 50

G

Gaddafi , Muammar, 16
Galbraith, J.K., 76
Garner , Jay, 19
General Agreement on Tariffs and
    Trade, 111, 146
General Agreement on Trade in
    Services, 66
Germany, 15
globalization, 60, 61-74, 147
    brainwashing, 64-65
    effects on poor countries, 66-71,
        73, 74
    of financial services, 99-102
    "good" and "bad," 62
    nation-states crippled, 62-64, 65,
        74-75, 116-119, 144-145
Globe and Mail, 93, 94, 96, 100,
    160, 176
Godsoe, Peter, 100
gold standard, 149
Goodbye Canada (Hellyer), 177
government-created money, 73-74,
    75, 81, 85, 92, 153-154, 166-167,
    176-178
    objections considered, 177-178
Granatstein, J.L., 137-138
Great Depression, 87
Great Lakes cleanup, 162
greed, 29-30, 84
Guantanamo Bay Naval Base, 36, 37
Guest, Brian, 168
Gulf War, 13-14

H

Halliburton company, 46-47
Harper, Stephen, 180
Harris, Mike, 165
health care, concerns and goals, 172
health care in Canada, 157-159
health care in U.S., 43-44
Heard, Geoffrey, 150
Hellyer, Paul, 61
Heritage Foundation (U.S. think
    tank), 65-66
hospital closings in Canada, 161

housing, affordable, 173
Hudson, Michael, 144-145
Hughes, Ann, 111
Hugo, Victor, 169
Hurtig, Mel, 115
Hussein, Saddam, 11, 13-14, 16, 149

I

illegal combatants, 36-37
income gap, 24, 45
    Canada vs. U.S., 121
indefinite incarceration, 35
Industry Canada study on
    employment, 120
inflation, 75, 77, 78, 169
    as objection to GCM, 177
Informetrica Ltd., 166
infrastructure
    concerns and goals, 174
    effects of cutbacks, 164
insurance companies bought by
    banks, 88
interest rates, 67, 79, 82, 150, 152,
    170-171
International Monetary Fund (IMF),
    67, 144, 154
    and developing world, 67, 70-71,
    73, 144
Iran, 150
Iraq, war against, 10, 11-20, 141
    brainwashing, 11, 17-18, 38
    civilian deaths, 18
    justifications for, 11-18, 38, 142
    post-war situation, 19-20
    real purposes, 150

J

Jefferson, Thomas, 1
Joint Plan Red, 22
justice, double standard in, 40-42

K

Kennedy, Edward M., 52, 55-56
Kennedy, John F., 52
Keynes, John Maynard, 76
Khadduri , Imad, 12
Kim Jong-il, 16
Kimball, Daryl, 57
Kucinich , Dennis J., 34-35, 139
Kurds, 13
Kyoto greenhouse gas reduction
    targets, 173

L

laissez-faire see economic
    fundamentalism
Landsberg , Michele, 9
Lapham , Lewis, 25
Lay , Kenneth, 31
Layton, Jack, 182-184
Leblanc, Daniel, 163
leverage
    capital adequacy for banks, 82-83
    leveraged buyouts, 84
Liberal Party of Canada, 179
Lincoln, Abraham, 83, 102
Lord, Bernard, 120
Los Angeles Times, 19
Lougheed, Peter, 114
Lukashenko , Alexander, 16

M

MacKay, Peter, 180
mad cow disease, 161
Maher , Bill, 39
Mandela, Nelson, 142
Manley, John, 95-96, 98, 114, 169
market fundamentalism *see* economic
    fundamentalism
"Marquess of Queensberry" Trade
    Rules, 146-147
Martin, Paul, 95, 157-168, 179
    cutbacks in 1995 budget, 160-166
    right-wing economics, 157, 159,
    167-168
McCallum, John, 138
McQuaig, Linda, 119
Medicaid health insurance, 43
mergers of banks, 90-101
Milhollin , Gary, 17
military buildup in U.S., 3, 47, 49-
    50, 138
    nuclear weapons, 56-57
    preventive wars, 54-56
    space weapons, 6, 36, 57-59
    weapons of mass destruction, 6, 56
military intervention, 140
military technology, 18
Miller , Brian, 32
Mining Watch Canada, 173
missile defences, 57-59
MMT case, 117
monetarist economics *see* Friedman,
    Milton

monetary policy and fiscal policy,
    171
money
    bank-created, 79-80, 81, 82-85,
        99, 154, 177-178
    effects of supply, 75-77, 154, 176
    government-created *see*
        government-created money
    paper money, 79, 80
    "virtual money," 82
moral compass, 33, 47
Morgan Stanley (U.S. firm), 29
Mugabe , Robert, 16
Mulroney, Brian, 82, 102, 110, 112,
    114, 120-121, 158
multilateralism, 139-140
multinational corporations, 25, 66,
    116-117

N
NAFTA, 115-122
    corporations vs. nations, 116-117
    energy security, 119
    impact on environment, 118
    supported by PCs, 179
    see also free trade; Free Trade
        Agreement
nation-states weakened, 62-64, 65,
    73-74, 116-119, 144-145
National Farmers Union on free
    trade, 105-108
"national interest" of U.S., 26-27
National Missile Defense, 58, 138
National Post, 114
National Security Strategy, 55
NATO, 1, 22, 136
neo-classical economics (neo-cons),
    62, 67
    in U.S. administration, 142, 143,
        150
    see also economic fundamentalism
Netanyahu, Benjamin, 11-12
New Democratic Party, 181, 182
New World Order, 3, 26, 62-63, 69,
    70, 146
New York Times, 5, 19-20, 44
Ney, Edward, 111
Nicholson, Peter, 159
Nixon, Gordon, 100
NORAD, 22, 136
nuclear weapons, 12, 16, 48, 54, 56-
    57

O
Observer, 13
O'Connor, Dennis, 161
Ogdensburg Agreement (1940), 22
oil, 18, 78, 147-148
O'Neil, Maurice, 164
Orchard, David, 180

P
Palast, Gregory, 64, 65, 70
Palestine, 8
paper money, 80
Parizeau, Jacques, 88
parliamentary committees on finance,
    95, 96-97
Patriot Act, 44
Paul, Ron, 143
peace, 3
peacekeeping, 139-140
Pearl Harbor, 10, 22, 55
Pearson, Lester B., 2, 126
Pentagon, 4-5
    and Iraq War, 12, 19
    military buildup, 3, 47, 49-50, 54-
        59
    surveillance system, 36, 45
    "war on terrorism," 9-10, 137, 138
    see also military buildup in U.S.
permanent government
    in Canada, 170
    in U.S., 25-27, 28
Peters, Doug, 158, 159
Peters, Erik, 160
Peterson , Peter G., 30
Pinochet , Augusta, 16
Poindexter , John, 36
poor people, 44, 50-51, 73, 148
poverty, 67
`pre-emptive' action, 54, 55
preventive wars, 54-56
privacy laws, 36
productivity and wages, 78
Progressive Conservative Party, 180
Project for a New American
    Century, 3-7, 10, 18, 22, 71, 137,
    140
provisional government in U.S., 27-
    29
public debt, 171-172
Purcell , Philip, 32
purchasing power, 76-77

Q

Québec, 183

R

Reagan, Ronald, 2, 22, 28, 63, 123
recessions of 1980s and 1990s, 78-79, 171
religious right, 52-55
reserve requirements, 80-81, 82-83, 90
revenge, 54-55
rich and poor, income disparity, 24, 44, 65
Ritter , Scott, 14, 17, 142-143
Rockefeller, David, 27
Roosevelt, Franklin D., 9, 22
Roosevelt, Teddy, 21
Royal Bank, 89, 92, 94, 99-100, 178
rules-based trading system, 144, 146-147, 155
Rumsfeld , Donald, 3, 18, 56-57
Russia, 15

S

Sacks, Jeffrey, 69
SARS, 160
Saudi Arabia, 8, 39, 150
Say's Law, 76
scandals, corporate, 31-33
Scrushy , Richard M., 44
S.D. Myers Inc. v. Canada, 117
Securities & Exchange Commission, 41, 44
securities dealers bought by banks, 87, 89
Shiller , Robert J., 45
Smetters-Gokhale study, 50
Smith, Adam, 73
soft-wood lumber dispute, 112
Soros, George, 74
Soviet Union, 1-2, 3, 136, 138
space weapons, 6, 36, 58, 168
Stiglitz, Joseph, 66, 71, 98, 144
Sunbelt Water Inc. v. Canada, 117
surveillance, 35-36, 46

T

Tanzania, 69
tar ponds at Sydney, Nova Scotia, 173
tariffs, and Free Trade Agreement, 112

tax breaks, 45
terrorism, 16
   "illegal combatants," 36-37
   World Trade Center attacked, 7-10, 18, 53-55
Terrorist Information Awareness, 36, 47
think tanks for right, 64-65
Third World see developing countries
Thomas, William, 149
"three strikes" law, 41
tolls, 174
Toronto District School Board, 164
Toronto Star, 95, 119, 161
torture, 54
Towers, Graham, 87
trade
   free see free trade; Free Trade Agreement; globalization; NAFTA
   rules-based system, 145, 146-147
transnational corporations, 25, 66
   corporations vs. nations, 116-117
transparency, 45-46
transportation, 174
Trilateral Commission (Trilats), 27
Trudeau, Pierre, 140
Truman, Harry S., 184
trust companies acquired by banks, 87, 89, 90
Turley , Jonathan, 37

U

unemployment
   and free trade, 119-120
   and recession of 1980s, 171
United Nations (U.N.), 14-15, 26, 140
United States
   constitutional violations, 34-37, 39-42
   election process, 28-29
   federal finances challenged, 50
   health care, 42-44
   investment in Canada, 111, 112-115
   military buildup, 3, 6, 47, 50, 55-62, 138
   neo-cons in administration, 143, 144, 151
   permanent government, 25-27, 28

plan *see* Project for a New
   American Century
relations with Canada, 20-23
religious right, 52-55
universities, 161-162

V

Vietnam War, 78, 136, 139
Volcker, Paul, 67, 68, 79, 152-153,
   171

W

wages and productivity, 78
Walkerton tragedy, 161
Wall Street, 31-33, 40-41, 54, 73
Wallin, Pamela, 114
War for Independence, 72-73
war on terrorism, 9-10, 52, 137, 138
Washington Consensus, 62, 67-68,
   73
water
   contamination, 118, 159, 160
   sale, 117
Waxman , Henry, 46
weapons of mass destruction
   development by U.S., 6, 57
   reason for Iraq War, 11-14, 16,
      38, 142
   supplied to Iraq by U.S., 12-13, 16
Wessel , David, 32
Weston, Galen, 178
Wilson, Michael, 89-90
Wolfowitz , Paul, 3, 38
World Bank, 64, 144-145, 155
   new world bank proposed, 151,
      155
   and Third World, 66-72, 152
World Trade Center attacked, 7-10,
   18, 51-53
World Trade Organization, 63, 66,
   145-146, 155
World Vision, 50
World War I, 21
World War II, 22, 83, 87, 176
WorldCom, 31-32

Y

Yedlin, Deborah, 161

Judy La Marsh

Memories of a bird
in a guilded cage

Memories of a lady.

Alexander Campbell
The Trouble re America
Int Lair writer — 1964 — 1970 New Republican
1932. S. Afr.
1950 Time Life
1961 Washing Correspondant
The Heart of India
      african
      Japan